The Art of
Teaching
Christianity

The Art of Teaching Christianity

Enabling the Loving Revolution

Wayne R. Rood

Photographs by Robert D. Fitch

Abingdon Press
Nashville & New York

THE ART OF TEACHING CHRISTIANITY

Copyright © 1968 by Abingdon Press

Library of Congress Catalog Card Number: 68-11472

Photographs on pp. 18, 80, 117, 146, and 212 are used
by permission of Glide Urban Center. The photograph on
p. 212 appeared in *Reluctant Revolution* by Arnold Come,
published by Glide Urban Center.

SET UP, PRINTED, AND BOUND BY THE
PARTHENON PRESS, AT NASHVILLE,
TENNESSEE, UNITED STATES OF AMERICA

A Note to the Reader

Education is the art of informing common sense with wisdom. Christian education is education informed by Christian love. And Christians believe that the loving presence of God in human life is so potent that if it were taken seriously the entire world would be refashioned.

These essays on the art of enabling that loving revolution began with a course at the College of Theology at Silliman University in the Philippine Islands in 1958-59. I was a long way from my library and files, and their content would probably not have been of much help to the students anyway. Usually I write out lectures fully, but that situation seemed to demand something special, and I found myself teaching from notes jotted on odd scraps of paper in what seemed to be moments of insight. Since then, some of the essays have been given a half-dozen times as a course in the Religious Education Department at the Pacific School of Religion in Berkeley, California. Others have been offered separately in teachers' meetings and conferences on the West Coast. In each instance, the pupils helped refine and clarify what I was thinking. The final writing was done in England at Oxford University, where the consciousness of a distinguished continuity of great teachers for eight centuries should have had some effect.

The basic principles were crystallized in my mind by two books which deserve special mention, each of them quite small and both of them quite great. With each of them I spent an entire summer in widely different places, both of which were for me schools of revolution. The first was the summer of 1945, during the battle for Okinawa. I was a chaplain with the 105th Infantry Regiment, and beside the Bible, one slim book comprised all the reading I found room for in my gear. It was John Macmurray's *The Structure of Religious Experience*. The other summer was ten years later, and the place was the delta area of the Niger River in West Africa, where I was investigating an indigenous religious movement. The book that summer, in addition to the same copy of the Bible, was Martin Buber's *I and Thou*.

There are no footnotes in these essays. That is not because I have not used sources, but because I have used so many. This prefatory Note must serve as a footnote to all that follows—rather inverted, of course, because it comes at the beginning and might therefore better be called a Headnote.

This Headnote would not be complete without a massive personal note to everyone I have ever met: family, teachers, pastors, buddies, authors, colleagues, classmates, students, friends and acquaintances have each taught me something, and some reflection of it appears somewhere in these pages.

Since so many good people are implicated in what follows, perhaps at least some of it will be interesting. More than that, I hope that you may personally be encouraged in the art of teaching-and-learning Christianity and enabling the loving revolution.

W.R.R.

Contents

1

The Nature of Teaching

Teaching is an almost universal activity of human beings.

Teaching Christianity is an art. This seems to be true, despite the
three-hundred-year-old suspicion among Protestants that religion
and art do not mix much better than oil and water. As an art,
teaching Christianity requires considerable active doing, in spite
of the American saying beginning, "Them as can, do." It is an art,

if only because of the part truth summed up in the aphorism, "Religion is caught, not taught." Like all arts, teaching requires highly refined skills, laying claim to the half-truth missed in the proverb, "Teachers are born."

Indeed, so much talent and skill are involved in practicing the art of teaching that one is tempted to apply to it the classic remark once directed against women's preaching which "is like a dog's walking on his hind legs. It is not done well; but you are surprised to find it done at all."

Nevertheless, teaching is done almost everywhere and always. One is tempted to say that it is like pelicans flying: the wonder is that it is not done better because it is done so much. It is done so much that man might be said to be "The Teaching Animal." Aristotle is credited with having invented the definition of man as "The Thinking Animal"; anthropologists have developed the claim that man is "The Talking Animal"; historians have proposed the notion that man is "The Developing Animal." The sum and completion of all these definitions might be that man is most characterized by that mysterious act called teaching, together with that corresponding and equally mysterious act called learning, and the union of these two acts in that meaning-developing, culture-shaping, person-producing relation called the teaching-learning process.

Almost anywhere that two or more human beings find themselves together for any length of time in any significant way, teaching and learning are going on, for wherever there are two persons there are differences between them, and these differences precipitate the sharing of information, know-how, wisdom, and experience in a giving-and-receiving exchange.

Difference in age is one of the most common sources of teaching-and-learning: the older possesses data and perspectives the younger has not yet achieved, the younger often entertains ideas and skills that are not yet tested but may provide fresh insight for the older wisdom. The situation in which the older and younger meet most directly and constantly is, in the modern world as it was in the ancient, the home.

When mother love responds to the baby's first cry and provides the infant with what he does not yet know he needs, when adult wisdom intercepts the child's random lurch toward a flame or a knife, the teaching process has begun. As soon as the baby begins to discover and accept the reason for avoiding the attractively shining object, the learning process has begun. And when the growing child begins to impose organic resistance to one kind of food and favor for another, the child has begun teaching. Therewith all the essential elements of the dynamic giving-and-receiving interchange have come into being—a minor wonder, perhaps, in view of the complex and disciplined educational situations some day to come. The lessons the parents and the children learn in the home are too numerous and perhaps too trivial to detail, but it seems certain that no social agency will ever surpass the home's capacity to instill personal habits, establish value systems, and communicate the wonders and limits of love.

Parents are, of course, not the only teachers in the home by mere virtue of age difference. It is sometimes the brother in the second grade who actually teaches the kindergarten child to read. It is frequently the adolescent sister who teaches the brother the meaning of discipline. Siblings may be the only ones who can really teach personal hygiene, the value of money, or the importance of being able to absorb a practical joke. It seems to be the role of grandparents rather than parents to pass on the cultural and family traditions, and sometimes grandchildren can only reveal to grandparents what they most need from their own parents.

Difference in experience is also a natural source of the teaching-and-learning experience. The guild system of teaching and learning the trades was based on the difference in persons created by experience: the master had labored long enough and achieved sufficient skill in his work to be able to show an apprentice how to do the job, and the journeyman had amassed enough experience to work on his own but not enough to introduce a beginner to the trade. Occasionally an apprentice learned so well and possessed so much talent that he literally leaped to mastership, and sometimes as legends affirm, the apprentice taught the master, the system being sufficiently appreciative of human differences to permit this leap. The principle that wide experience qualifies one person to teach another of less experience still governs the learning of many modern trades. Shop workers, foremen, and production managers; clerks, secretaries, and executives; recruits, drill sergeants, and commanding officers: all have been taught and are teaching others and are learning from others.

Difference in knowledge is a recognized source of teaching-and-learning. The medical doctor possesses a specialized knowledge of the functions of the human body and the evidences of its malfunction. He sometimes uses this knowledge to put things right; he often uses it to teach the patient what the patient does not know but desperately needs to know to help the process of healing and to keep things right; he frequently depends on the patient to teach him the peculiarities of his individually sick body. The relationship between psychiatrist and patient, lawyer and client, advertiser and public, salesman and buyer, mechanic and motorist, politician and electorate is usually a teaching-and-learning relationship dependent upon the fact that each knows something about the immediate situation that both need.

The essence of teaching-and-learning thus appears to permeate human life. We all teach. We do it much of the time. We all learn, and we do that, too, a great deal. Both teaching and learning interpenetrate our living. We do not expect, therefore, to find the process basically extraordinary or exotic. It is not merely universal, however, and therefore relatively unidentifiable and meaningless. It is dependent upon the differences between human beings, and these must be significant enough to be noted and acted upon by both parties. That means that it is a dynamic process, which is to say that both teachers and learners are active in it, and that sometimes their roles are reversed as the process develops.

Often it has seemed productive to establish some control over this natural, universal relationship of sharing caused by important human differences. When that is done, the familiar accoutrements of educational institutions quickly appear: schools, subjects, schedules, and specialists. Usually it is said by the society that the school system was created in the interests of efficiency, sometimes that the society had lessons to teach that the family or the family physician could not teach as well. In either case, the informal teaching-and-learning of human relationships became formal education.

Formal education adds consciousness to informal teaching-and-learning. Many of the lessons of the home and the shop occur without awareness; this is sometimes said, usually by harassed parents or by romantic philosophers of education, to be the strength of informal education, and it may well be so: informal teaching is usually not strengthened by deliberation. Formal education, on the other hand, implies a conscious attempt by the teacher to be as effective a teacher as he possibly can. This usually implies a conscious preparation by the teacher, deliberately heightening his skill and information. It is usually thought to be advantageous if the pupils, also, become aware of the process, and consciously attempt to become as effective learners as they possibly can. This awareness of tasks and roles in the process is usually—though not always—aided by consciously designating a place, a time, and a content: a schoolroom equipped to inspire and facilitate learning; regular hours for instruction and study; subjects suitable for study in these conditions. In the interests of efficiency, it is assumed that these facilities must

15

be designed so as to make it possible for the conscious teacher to teach a number of conscious learners at once: the classroom will be large enough to accommodate two or three dozen students, the hours long enough to extend learning to the limit, the content of the sort permitting group mastery and memorization.

The shift from informal teaching-and-learning to formal education need not be merely dismal, of course, and, in any case, in a complex society and modern world it is necessary. It is clear, however, that it brings about an emphasis on the teacher as the central actor in the educational process at the expense of emphasis on the pupil as an active participant, on rigid if elegant equipment at the cost of flexibility and development, and on facts, rules, and skills at the price of values, attitudes, and individuality. It will never be possible, probably, to return to the once cherished ideal of "Mark Hopkins on one end of the log and the student on the other," but modern mass education will probably be able to improve its quality only as it discovers effective ways of vitalizing the fragile values of the informal teaching-and-learning relation.

The difference between "knowledge of" and "knowledge about" has already been suggested and needs to be clarified, if possible. Knowledge of a subject is usually associated with the informal teaching-and-learning process, knowledge about a subject with formal education. The difference is by no means as simple as positive and negative, though some philosophers of education would make it seem so, and the solution of the problem posed is therefore not merely to choose between them.

"Knowledge of" is direct in nature and achieved indirectly by association. Its content is immediately experienced, emotionally felt, and usually nonverbally expressed. It is of the nature of flesh-and-blood, but not merely of the self. It is knowledge of how things feel on the inside rather than about how they appear on the outside, knowledge of everything as identified with oneself, but not merely subjective. It is individual, singular, profound, and secretive, but not merely subconscious. It is spiritual and intuitive, but not merely otherworldly or aesthetic. It deals with attitudes, convictions, and emotions and results in decision and action. It is the sort of knowledge from which art and its mysteries emerge.

"Knowledge about" is achieved directly by observation and refined through its deductive consequences, but it never knows the inside, the actual nature of things. It is knowledge about things, physical events, and moral behavior from the outside. It is satisfactorily reducible to objective assertions of fact, and this is one of the tests of truth. It is of the nature of the objective world, other than the knower, implacable, unaffected by wish. It is hard-nosed, universally true if true at all. It is observable, measurable, manipulatable. It deals with information, data, statistics, and labels, and it results in theory and description. It is the sort of knowledge on which science and its wonders are built.

"Of" and "about" are not mutually exclusive in nature, but it is the educator's tendency to treat them as if they were separate. No education will be complete unless its pupils learn to value and handle both. Because formal education by its nature tends to emphasize "knowledge about," and informal teaching-and-learning by its nature tends to emphasize "knowledge of," it is the danger of formal education that it tends inevitably to substitute "about" for "of." It is the task, therefore, of formal education, whatever its institutions, to learn the art of insinuating "knowledge of" into its program of teaching "knowledge about."

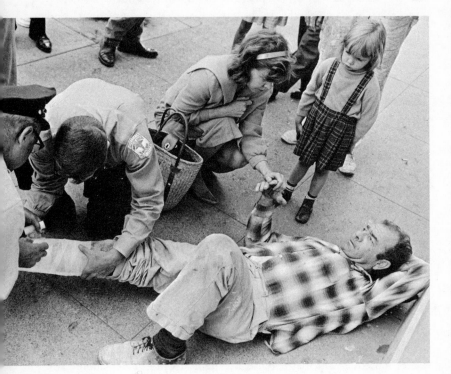

2

The Content of Christianity

Teaching Christianity is not unlike teaching anything else.

It is also different from teaching anything else. Presumably it should be pointed out that this is a paradox. It is true, however, not for that reason, but because of the nature of the special content of Christianity which forces a new dimension into the teaching-and-learning relation. The content of Christianity, like that of history and literature, for example, contains facts, relations, and concepts to be known about. That content is taught and learned, when it is done well, very much like effective teaching and learning of history and literature. Unlike mathematics and science, for example, it also carries a content of feeling, response, and behavior that can only be known of. That content is taught and learned very much unlike the content of mathematical and scientific subjects.

But that is not the end of the difference, for the content of the Christian faith possesses a peculiar character which requires its teaching and learning to be unique. For this mysterious fact the teacher of Christianity is often prone to cry "Vive la différence!" or "Praise the Lord!" according to his literary tastes. And sometimes he is overwhelmed by the fact and may exclaim "What kind of fool am I!" or "Lord, be merciful to me, a sinner!"

The content of the Christian faith is unique in education because it conveys the revelation of God. The content of revelation is not a series of ideas or concepts to be placed alongside others in equations or formulas. Revelation means that God wants to be known —not known about or even known of. It is a self-revelation, initiated by God and carried through by God. Indeed, it is inaccurate to speak of the content of revelation as if God were contained therein as some inert datum: revelation is God acting; the content is God addressing and offering himself to men. Though it is worth remembering that this may be said also of the content of history or mathematics, the meaning of that statement is defined by reference to the presence of God in self-revelation. In much more than a metaphorical sense, therefore, God is in the content of the Christian faith. Indeed, it may not be inappropriate to say that God is the content. There is, of course, much in the formal statements of the Christian institutions that has little to do with this unique content. That is precisely why Horace Bushnell pointed

19

out in a commencement address over a hundred years ago to his own theological school that the proper object of the study of theology is divinity, not theology.

The content of the Christian faith transcends not only the "about" and "of" dichotomy, but also the "objective" and "subjective" antithesis. In this content, God's acts are objective and the results of his acts in the individual person are subjective. God speaks, and his words possess me and I possess them. For the purposes of teaching and learning, it is probably necessary to open this union and deal with the objective facts of ancient history, the life and sayings of Jesus, the development of doctrine, the martyrdom of the saints, and the evangelization of the world. To do this requires all the best techniques of teaching facts. But it is worth doing for the teacher of Christianity, not only because these objective data carry with them the lively potentiality of personal seizure by the meaning of the facts. The purpose of teaching Christianity is, after all, not persuasion, though the teacher may be brilliantly convincing, but conversion, a relationship to God in which it might be said that the objective and subjective are combined.

The content of Christianity is special, further, because it is creative of its own acceptance. God discloses himself—infinite, eternal, holy, absolute. The disclosure is to man—finite, mortal, sinful, relative. Man is quite incapable of knowing God as he really is, for human experience gives no basis for understanding divine qualities. God, nevertheless, yearns to be known; he wills himself across the differences between himself and man; his act literally creates in man the acceptance of that which is beyond man's understanding and capacity. This is precisely the reason that so much of religious biography, and of theology for that matter, seems to be inarticulate when it comes to the major point: the entire situation is, by nature, beyond understanding, and therefore "trans-verbal." And this is, in turn, the reason that exclusive dependence on verbal communication in teaching Christianity is often so in-effective—preaching, theologizing, lecturing, and the writing of books, are by nature verbal appeals to the mind, whereas the content itself is by nature a trans-verbal appeal to the whole person. The ultimate reason that verbalizing is successful at all is that God is acting in the content of Christianity, creating its acceptance in man.

The content of Christianity is peculiar, thus, in that it carries its own imperative. Because God enables the revelation to be received, this is a content about which its teachers do not have the right to decide whether or not it shall be communicated or kept to oneself or made obscure and objective. This is a content which must be shared, even though it be independent of this teacher's teaching. If he does not teach, someone or something else will, "the stones will cry out," or—perhaps even more embarrassing—the content may be communicated in spite of that teacher's effort and even though he has no understanding of what is happening. In short, Christians, and even some who do not consider themselves to be Christian, have no choice but to teach. This may constitute the best possible argument for doing it as well as possible.

As a result of this special nature of the content of Christianity, the nature of the teaching and learning roles is altered. The teacher, who is probably older in age than the learners, who has had more experience than they, who knows more facts, inevitably comes to the moment when he joins the learners as a learner of the revelation —in the presence—of God. All teachers are learners, too, of course, whatever their subject matter, but in most formal education it is helpful to keep the roles of teaching and learning distinct; in the teaching of Christianity, however, the actual mark of success in teaching is the surrender of the teaching role to the content. To do this requires a trust of both the content and the learners beyond that ordinarily expected of teachers, and in this case made possible by the content itself.

The teaching of Christianity is thus like all teaching, but moves significantly beyond into what may be considered a different dimension.

There is a kind of teaching in which the *teacher* carries the *content* to the *learner*. The teacher is the active person in this relationship,

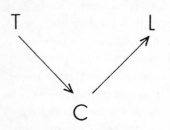

and his activity is the ground of the process: whatever life is possessed by the content is given it by the teacher. The result is good inasmuch as the teacher is good, that is to say, persuasive, entertaining, clever, the master of the content and of the learners. It is sometimes called "transmissive" education, and the lecture is the usual method of teaching. It is thought to be old-fashioned, but classical education and university courses usually proceed upon this concept. So do many church school classes.

There is another kind of teaching in which the *teacher* and the *learner* meet in the *content*. The content may be thought of as

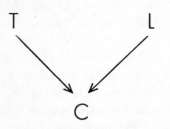

inert, or passive; it is usually comprised of objective data and facts. No direct meeting of persons is implied, but teacher and learners relate to each other in regard to the content and in terms of its nature. Both the teacher and the learner are active and approach the content together. The content itself is the ground of the process. A good example of this form of teaching may be the debate or, in less formal teaching-and-learning, the mediation of a dispute.

A third form of teaching-and-learning is characterized by a direct meeting between the *teacher* and the *learners,* without regard to objective *content*. Indeed, the content is this case is the self of the teacher and of the learners. The selves also comprise the ground of the process. Initiative and activity are required of both parties. "Discussion" and "therapy groups" would be illustrations of this form. Much so-called progressive education has moved in this direction, and it has had quite a vogue in church schools. A great deal of learning about the self—one's own and others' as well—is often achieved. It sometimes degenerates into mere mutual admiration groups, and the dangers in regard to the teaching of Christianity in this fashion are superficiality and subjectivism.

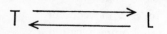

A fourth form combines the teaching and learning functions and has been provocatively described and advocated by Martin Buber. The ground of the process is the *teacher's* active concern—love—for both the *learner* and the *content*. The teacher endeavors to "step over to the other side" of the relationship, to "see" or "experience" the content from the learner's point of view. This act, freely ventured by the older and wiser, enlists a response from the learner who joins the teacher in the process. The response of the learner is to both teacher and content, and both teacher and learner become learners in relation to a shared content which is no longer objective but has become personalized by love. This relation is more dynamic than any of the foregoing, and it is based in a warm and creative Judaic philosophy.

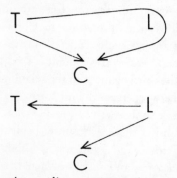

When the content is the Christian gospel, a new dimension is thrust into the situation, for in this instance the content is active, as well as the teacher and the learners. Indeed, the content is the ground of the communication, reaching to teacher and learners independently and initially. The *teacher,* knowing the *gospel content* and motivated by it, reaches to the *learner.* Thus both the content and the teacher are active, and draw response and participation from the

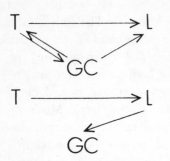

learners. This might be called "Communication of the Gospel." A significant increase in dynamic is to be seen here, related to but not quite the same as Buber's concept because in this view the content is independently active and meaningful.

Christians, both laymen and theologians, are very much aware of a vertical dimension in Christian experience called "encounter." When the content is God, the third element in the relation between teacher and learner is not only active but personal and creative. Encounter begins with *God* addressing both *teacher* and *learner.* Each has some reply to make. The teacher has replied, and this prior reply becomes the ground of communication between himself and the learners. This double relationship with the learner becomes, in turn, the

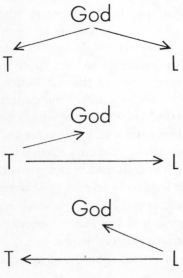

ground of the learner's response. Thus the interrelationship is completed in the vertical dimension. This relation is reminiscent of the third form, but inserts into the wholly horizontal relation between two human beings Kierkegaard's insistence that "God is always the middle tèrm" in human relations, according to the Christian understanding.

However, this description of encounter is purely theoretical, for actually the gospel content is always in the situation, also. Though much formal theology would make it seem that encounter can take place and be understood *in vacuo,* and though most educational philosophy would seem to suggest that the teaching of Christianity can take place only on the humanistic level of Buber's concept or the horizontal level of communication of the gospel, they cannot in actual experience be so separated or explained. To begin to glimpse something, though through a glass darkly, of what is actually going on in teaching Christianity, it is necessary to pile up the last three concepts, keeping in mind the actual functions of the preceding three. In teaching Christianity, the *teacher* begins in a

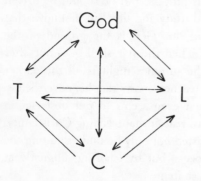

situation already alive with *God's* address to all persons individually and already containing the special *content.* His own initial response, partial and misunderstood though it may unfortunately be, impels him to lay his knowledge and concern at the disposal of the *learner,* to "cross over," to become catalyst for the learner's response. That initial response may be to the teacher, to the content, or to God, but that is immaterial because it becomes the enabler of the other two responses, and all three reinforce one

25

another, and complete the total growing experience. The teacher's method is not primarily lecture nor discussion nor relationship, but rather the effort to feel the situation "whole" and to deal with content, relation, and response in the fashion his talents enable. For the sake of structure, it might be worth suggesting that the God-ward movements might be labeled "worship," the content-centered ones "study," and the horizontal ones "life."

It is now necessary to stretch the imagination into a third dimension—for which no diagram shall here be attempted—because this last diagram is merely individual and therefore "flat": all this actually takes place in the context of others in the same situation, the community of followers and seekers, the *koinonia*.

With this insight, the dynamism and complexity that have been accumulating step by step may burst like a fireworks rocket into the night sky. With all this going for us, how can we fail? The teacher of Christianity ought to be the happiest warrior of them all, as, indeed, he has been in some of the most spectacular moments of Christian history. His best is not a good enough ticket to admit him to participation in this mysterious process, and he should be driven to a deep plunge into worship and study and life. But he knows that whatever he offers can be useful, for God is the ground of the process in which he is involved. Then the star shell goes out after its instant of illumination and the summer night is all the darker for its moment of brilliance. The teacher knows that he, nevertheless, does fail to do his best and often even seems to put obstacles in the way of the process. It is for this reason that teaching Christianity, like teaching anything else, is assisted not only by understanding the role the teacher plays in the process, but by laboring diligently at the skills of teaching this special content.

3

The Nature of Teaching Christianity

The art of teaching Christianity is the art of enabling dialogue.

Unfortunately, dialogue is rapidly becoming a smooth word in the English language. To describe something as noteworthy and diamond-bright as teaching Christianity, a clear and sharp word is needed. But we round words off by using them. Like coins, they can be kept in circulation so long and used so much that they become worn smooth, and finally they look so much one like the other that it is difficult to determine their value or even the country from which they came. In the course of time, we even change their meaning: "let" once meant to prevent, and now it usually means to permit. "Marvelous" is employed—usually along with another smooth word, "Darling"—in approval of a lady's gown, when, in fact, the actual meaning of the word might be both more accurate and less approving: "extravagantly improbable." "Fabulous," originally referring to fables, becomes descriptive of an evening distinguished only by an absence of boredom, "fantastic" of a moderately good play. Even an important word like "redemption"—redolent of medieval serfs and manors and used to explain the Atonement—is borrowed by the trading stamps company and applied to the shop where stamps may be turned in by the tattered bookful for little-wanted "gifts"—the only Redemption Center in town that is open on weekdays now that the midweek prayer meeting has gone out of style.

Only a short time ago, dialogue was a sharp word. It is rooted in a Greek word in two parts meaning "conversation across" and has traceable family connections through Latin, Old French, and Middle English. In 20th-century English, it had come to refer chiefly to the conversations of novels and playscripts. However, Martin Buber dug the concept out of the Hebraic past and cut and polished it for at least two generations of theologians and philosophers. For him dialogue is a living, mutual relation. The foundations of his usage are most available in *I and Thou,* the applications in *Between Man and Man;* the concept is also to be found in all his philosophical works, and it is extensively illustrated in his volumes of Hasidic tales.

Dialogue is, for Buber, the fulfillment of this fragile existence between birth and death which we call human life. All phenomena are either personal or nonpersonal, "Thou" or "It," and all human experience is either *I-Thou* or *I-It* in nature. The moral imperative of this distinction is that *Thous* shall never be treated as *Its*. The characteristic of human life is the capacity to relate directly to *Thous*. The creative possibility of human existence is to discover and relate to *The Thou* in every *Thou* and, further, in any *It*. Thus do I become *Thou* in my own being. Because we live in a world of *Thous*, we are constantly being addressed in thought and speech and action. For the most part, however, we do not listen to the address, or we break into it with meaningless chatter: we treat *Thous* as if they could be ignored; even worse, we manipulate and use *Thous*, as we manipulate and use *Its*, thus denying life and fulfillment to those *Thous* and to ourselves as well. But, when the address comes to us and the answer proceeds from us, then human life actually exists, though brokenly, in the world. The kindling of "that spark of the soul," the "blazing up of the response," is our responsibility as persons. The educator is the chosen "ambassador" of this responsibility. Education is offering, through the medium of a person (the teacher), a selection of the world for the response of another person (the learner), and the encouragement of that response by the teacher who voluntarily leaves his own individuality to "cross over" to the student's side of life, "to experience the pupil's being educated." This influencing of the lives of others with one's own life—"otherwise to be found only as grace, inlaid in the folds of life"—in education becomes a function and a law. Thus by intentionally bringing the pupil to his own unity, the teacher will help "to put him again face to face with God."

The poetic profundity and philosophical polish of this meaning of dialogue perhaps pervades even this prosaic condensation of it. Faced with such a big word, we usually tend to cut it down to our own size, round it off so that it can trip easily off the tongue, and, we hope, impressively. We make it useless by using it too easily and too much. It was noticed that it bore a resemblance to another precious word of the thinkers, "dialectic," and it was turned into an abstract and logical concept—much easier to handle than an existential and mystical experience. Soon the derivative form "dialogical" was in use, which could be a fuzzy and comfortable substitute for the more technical and demanding word "dialectical." Now it is in the popular domain, and "dialogue" has been used to designate a method of conducting discussion groups, as a name for a retreat house, and, perhaps completing its deterioration, as a verb. However, because sometimes the most effective way to a goal is through the dangers and taking advantage of them, the course here will be "Damn the Torpedoes: Full Steam Ahead!" The word is *dialogue:* it will be used as a banner around which to rally an approach to teaching Christianity that may be productive as well as courageous and adventuresome.

To do this, even at the further danger of distorting the banner into shapelessness, it is necessary to associate with it some other concepts.

The first of these is "love," not in the sense of class B movies and newspaper headlines, but in the radical biblical sense, wherein it is defined by God's acts with and for men. It is *agape,* as contrasted to *eros* or *philia,* the love that does not seek to possess the loved but to enable in him a love of the same kind. This love is not different from, but inclusive of, wrath, for in God it appears that judgment has exactly the same purpose as love: to create love. This is the relation the prophets thundered about, Paul sang about, and Jesus was. Since this love is addressed by God to every man, the possibility of becoming a loving person is constantly within and among us.

The concept of "person" will be used here to mean "agent in relation." John Macmurray, in an original Scottish combination of the moods of European existentialism and American pragmatism, turns Descartes's *cogito, ergo sum* right side up at last: *I act, therefore we are.* Action is man's irreducible and primal function as an individual, and thinking is a reflecting and abstract mode of being. To be a person is to be in dynamic acting-and-reflecting mutual relation with all things—objective, subjective, corporate, and divine.

The same essential elements define "experience," another concept to be drawn into the meaning of dialogue. In the huge body of his work, and especially in *Democracy and Education* and *Art as Experience,* John Dewey, *the* philosopher of experience, often calls it "the result," "the sign," "the reward" of that interaction of organism and environment which, when carried to the full, is a transformation of interaction into participation and communication. For Dewey, it all begins with animal fear of what life may bring forth, and with man's capacity consciously to unify the flow of events into meaning. Education is the reconstitution of experience for more effective experiencing. Art is the completion of experience through imagination and expression to enable unhindered communication between man and man in a world full of gulfs and walls that limit community of experience.

"Encounter" is a concept that is needed here because it is *the* word of a form of Christian theology emphasizing the "against-ness" installed by man into his relation with God and the resultant explosive quality of the reuniting of man with God. It is perhaps preeminently Emil Brunner's contribution in a dozen books: *Begegnung,* a coming together which implies the impact of moving into contact out of distance and estrangement, a unity in which the formal subject-and-object dichotomy of philosophy is transcended and *Wahrheit* (truth) emerges, a creative meeting of finite and infinite in the incarnation in which Jesus Christ appears for the salvation of men. It is also a useful concept in regard to communication between men, as used by Roger Mehl in his little book entitled

31

La rencontre de l'autrui. What is called communication, he observes, takes place at many levels and in many varieties, most of them superficial, casual, ambiguous; communication, however, is defined by that relationship in which there is actual contact, *encounter with the other,* even collision, a meeting "from eye to eye and from heart to heart."

Hendrik Kraemer, Eugene Nida, and others center on the word "communication" and the question whether it is possible to make the incomprehensible kerygma comprehensible to the secular understanding of life, to translate and vitalize it in such a way that it is at least recognized as relevant to the real needs of modern man who seems to thrive so excellently without God. Translation is a massively difficult task, says Nida, because of the technical problems of carrying Christian concepts into language meaningful for people who have no experiential basis in their dialects for understanding them; it may be a vain task, says Kraemer, because communication does not create community but depends upon it and there is a worldwide breakdown of community in the modern world. "Community" is another of the concepts to be gathered into the notion of dialogue. It, too, is currently being devalued by application to all sorts of associations of human beings from the nonpersonal life of housing projects to the purely formal and often strained working relationships of regional groups of armed forces: community is not a bundling together of individuals in physical proximity but a dynamic forcing together toward the common purpose of universal dialogue. It is an important word, treasured and courageously preserved by the early Christians under the Greek name "koinonia." With it should come the more active word from the same root, "communion," standing for the practice of an organic harmony between man and man or between man and the world which gallantly refuses to recognize barriers and separations that might destroy the relation if even admitted, a voluntary subordination of individuality in the interests of relation, a *Wirhaftigkeit,* a "we-feeling." This fellow-ship is so rare and so demanding that it cannot but be celebrated when visualized or realized. The Christian community celebrates communion, the fellowship of all things in God. The Christian teacher needs to understand that such communion is part of dialogue, and its celebration a function of the art of teaching.

With these depths and reaches of meaning gathered into the one word "dialogue" and added to what has been inferred in the first two chapters about the nature of teaching and the special content of Christianity, it is possible to suggest what is meant by it when it defines the teaching-and-learning of Christianity.

Dialogue (the teaching-and-learning of Christianity) is *personal.* As the philosophers would say, dialogue attaches to persons as persons; it is something that characterizes their existence. The Christian position is that men are persons because they are related to God who is, if not The Person, at least the Ground of personal Being. That relatedness is here called dialogue and is thought of as the address of God to man and man's response to it. The address has already been made, for God precedes man upon every scene. Man has no choice whether to respond, but he does decide the nature of his response. Decision is now being identified by many theistic and nontheistic thinkers as the most intensely personal act there is. On the human level, dialogue is an opportunity offered by one man to another to be personal, that is, to decide how to respond. Thus both participants are becoming persons and the resulting dialogue is a personal act.

Dialogue (the teaching-and-learning of Christianity) involves *distance.* There are chasms between persons. The current literature of theology, philosophy, and sociology is full of illustrations of the forces in modern culture that alienate men from one another, from their society, from their physical world, indeed, from themselves. There are also the differences of age, experience, and knowledge built into life which characterize all teaching-and-learning. Chasms do not need to be opened, they are everywhere; they do need to be discovered and understood. Men are bound together by the limits imposed by interhuman distances. Sometimes the distances between men expose them to God. There is therefore an "against-ness" in all teaching, sometimes a sense of combat, and it is often productive of the best teaching-and-learning. The chasms cannot be closed; however, a line is to be thrown across, a thin thread of love which sustains dialogue. For Christians, the model is, again, God's revelation: "God is in his heaven and you are on the earth," warns Karl Barth, and so it is that the chasm between infinite and finite is not to be eliminated but bridged by direct relation.

Dialogue (the teaching-and-learning of Christianity) requires *movement*. There is no movement without change, as Aristotle makes clear, but it need not be observable in space. Movement may be an inner act of change in attitude or intention, and it may be so real as to be accompanied by a tension of the muscles, a quickening of the pulse, and a salt taste. Change means movement into the unknown, a venture of faith. Dialogue involves actual acts of love and faith and is in two parts.

The first movement is initiative, and it is an act of love. Since the chasms are always present, someone must take the risk of acting first from his side. Man did not invite the incarnation; God acted, "in the fullness of time," and offered the world his Son, taking the implicit and ultimately actualized risk that men would not accept either the act or its reason. There could be no dialogue among men had not God taken initiative from the beginning of time; there will be no dialogue among men unless one of them reaches across to the other, offers to stand beside him in his place of living and suffering and achieving. The reality of the chasm means that the offer may be rejected or perverted or misinterpreted. The initiator must take that risk; he must also take care that it is not his initiative that precludes response or invites misinterpretation. Attentive listening or silent sharing may be a more effective invitation to dialogue than a torrent of words. For dialogue no sound is necessary. All great teachers have been listeners and watchers, often inviting response by their sheer awareness.

The second movement is response, and it is an act of faith. In daily life we are prone to mistake monologue for dialogue. It seems to be easy to ignore the fact that the other has not responded or even been listening. An address is necessary, but there is no dialogue without a reply. It takes two to converse as well as to tango. The response, in fact, may be more significant and difficult than the invitation, for it may well be that for the responder dialogue is a strange and threatening possibility. The history of the relation between Yahweh and the ancient Hebrews, between Jesus and his apostles, is a measure of the difficulty man finds in responding. The most personal and intimate act there is is to choose to respond. It is therefore worth waiting for and understanding even in the act of invitation. There are so many barriers and inhibitions in modern life to be overcome that response is a skill to be cultivated.

Dialogue (the teaching-and-learning of Christianity) requires *content*. Content is the link that holds the persons together. They cannot simply commune with their projections of one another's personalities. God's address to man was a *Word,* an incarnation, a Man-among-men. The Word was, of course, much more than a sound or an idea: it was an act full of meaning, "a lamp unto my feet," "a light unto my path"—a thing-in-itself that partook of and represented a thing-beyond-itself that was greater-than-itself. The establishment and maintenance of dialogue between human beings appears to depend upon a content that reaches through the particulars of individual experience to the universals—"the ultimate concerns"—joy, freedom, and truth, anxiety, guilt, and estrangement. Words and symbols help to frame this dialogue-shaping content, but the teacher of Christianity needs to beware lest the search for words and symbols obscure the fact that the content which ultimately supports dialogue is not a sign, but the presence of God himself.

Dialogue (the teaching-and-learning of Christianity) is *creative*. Because it is initiated by the acts of God, the Creator, dialogue creates its own acceptance. This is a mystery pointed to, but not explained by, the Christian doctrine of Grace. Since it is creative in nature and content, dialogue, even in human hands, is creative, also. The teacher will discover that, as he involves himself in the process of dialogue, he finds within himself talents and resources he never knew he had, and, more disturbing, that he is involved in activities and risks he never dreamed of undertaking. It is the further occupational hazard of the Christian teacher that the learner to whom he offers the possibility of dialogue may do far more with it than he ever dreamed of or produced himself. Dialogue is therefore not only the art of translation or of transmission; it is a method of discovery, a learning process for everyone involved in it.

Dialogue (the teaching-and-learning of Christianity) is *redemptive*. The entire biblical content is evidence that the divine purpose and achievement in relating himself to man is man's salvation. Although for many reasons it is important to keep clear the fact that the redemptive relationship between God and man is not transferable from one man to another, it is also important to keep clear the fact that dialogue between human beings is redemptive because God is active "where two or three are gathered together" in his name, rendering the interhuman dialogue contributory to the divine-human dialogue. How this works is a mystery symbolized but not explained by the doctrine of the Holy Spirit. To note this possibility is to warn that wherever dialogue is entered into in the presence of God, spiritual healing, emotional reorientation, and moral redirection may take place. The teacher of Christianity must be prepared to participate in this possibility.

This is the sort of dialogue into which the teacher of Christianity enters and into which it is his task to enable others to enter. Enabling is an art. Given the common talent possessed by everyone to be human beings, anyone who cares to try can learn to practice it.

4

Learners

Pupils are persons needing and seeking dialogue.

They come in an infinite variety of sizes, shapes, and dispositions —large, medium, and petite; pencil, pear, and potato shaped; eager, suspicious, and resistant. They are noisy, they stare, they avert their eyes. They are silent, they smile, they try to please in unimportant ways. There are empty faces, there are expectant faces, there are masks. And there is an almost imperceptible thunder: Who are *you*? Do *you* know something that concerns me? Do *you* bring me something? What do *you* bring? Why are *you* here? And there is another theme that promises to turn the faint rumble into music: Why am *I* here? Is there something *I* need to know? Is there something here to help *me*? What can it be? *Who am I?* They are questing for fulfillment, wanting knowledge, reaching for love.

They are more, however, than a chaotic bundle of half-asked questions and unformed possibilities. They are persons, they have histories, they exist in the world. They have been addressed by God and are, even now, moment-by-moment choosing their responses. They have already known achievement, joy, and failure. They come from homes, schools, and jobs. They are the products of complex relationships. They are centers of constantly changing relationships. They are learning beings.

For the teacher, each of them is the most important person in the classroom. Every teacher is, therefore, a student of students.

*

A person is the product of complex relationships.

There is apparently no such thing as an isolated human being. Psychology observes that without relationship the human infant would not survive. Philosophy proposes that the idea of an isolated person is self-contradictory: "I" exist only as one element of the complex "You and I." Formally stated, "I" am one term in the relation "You and I" which constitutes both the "You" and the "I." "No man is an island," wrote John Donne, and Christopher Fry adds detail: "Whatever happens on the farthest pitch, to the sand man in the desert or the island man in the sea, concerns me very soon." The prehistoric Hebrew poet pictured the Lord God forming the physical body of man from the dust of the ground, and then he "breathed into his nostrils the breath of life; and man became a living being."

Biologists and some psychologists explain that the homo sapiens is the product of a special set of successful adjustments to the forces and threats of the physical environment. John Dewey felt that conscious human experience began in an animal fear of the physical forces that threaten to overwhelm biological life and that man became a problem-solving human being when he applied imagination and intelligence to surmount the threat. The physical world is ambivalent in regard to human life: it may threaten or aid, it is both ugly and beautiful, it is alternately violent and peaceful. It is productive, however, of man's characteristic life, and is to be received gratefully, treated with respect, and responded to with as much sensitivity and knowledge as possible. The pupil is a product of this balance of forces in a delicately individual way.

A person is also the product of an inner relationship to self. Depth psychology has presented a vivid picture of the internal dramas of selfhood: self-and-other, male-and-female, conscious-and-subconscious. Developmental psychology has added another picture of the inner story with its consciousness of the pressures of physical growth, organic maturation, mental expansion. Religious psychology has explored the themes of freedom-and-authority, anxiety-and-certainty, guilt-and-redemption. The pupil is a multi-dimensioned, inner-developing, interrelating self.

A person is also formed in relationship to a series of small, face-to face, intimate groups of individual persons. The field of interpersonal relationships at the level of primary groups has been explored by students of group therapy and group dynamics. They have shown how dependent the human person is on direct human relationships for attitudes, values, and growth—indeed, even for survival in a radically competitive society. They have described the forces creating the long-recognized influence of the home, friendships, childhood gangs, work groups, and interest groupings, on the drama of individuality and mutuality in human development. The pupil in the classroom is an active participant in several primary groups, and they influence him significantly.

A person is further shaped by the specific culture and subcultures of the society in which he lives. Social and economic theory make vivid the pushes and pulls on the individual constantly exerted by the community, the economic class, the ethnic heritage, the national ethos, the language structure, and so on. Every person is engaged in a drama of past and future, limits and possibilities, individuality and conformity, as he lives out his task of discovering who he is and wants to be in society. The pupil, whether he be young or old, is engaged in this drama; some of the scenes are the same as those of the teacher, and some are very different.

A person is also the product of his relationship with God. Theologians are as much interested in the nature of this religious experience as they are in maintaining creedal orthodoxy, for it is from the experience that creeds arose in specific times and circumstances. Like all the other levels of the self-drama, the religious relationship may be positive or negative, productive or destructive, depending upon individual responses. In a way, God is as much to be adjusted to as the forces of the physical world, and individuality is as much shaped by the nature of these responses as by one's adjustment to primary groups or to society.

Both teachers and learners are persons and the individual products of these interacting relationships. From his own position in the complex drama of interrelationships, the teacher reaches out to the pupil in his drama, not in an attempt to understand him, for that

41

is always a secret and sacred mystery, but in the humble effort to experience what it might mean to stand beside him in his individuality.

*   *

A person is also a center of constantly changing relationships.

For the teacher it is especially important to have some sense of the sweep of ordinary life from birth to death, and some special understanding of the specific age level of his pupils. If they are adolescents or younger, books of educational psychology will guide the teacher with generalizations about reading skills, range of interests, the kinds of facts and relations the pupil's mind can grasp. In addition, the teacher will need to have a view of the pupil's stance in life in regard to the capacity for and skills of dialogue. Change, both growth and deterioration, seems to characterize both the human life-span and its individual events. There is reason to think that change is the result of the continuously creative acts of God. Learning to cope with new circumstances or make something out of them seems to characterize human personality. There is reason to suspect that this capacity to grapple with life is evidence of the image of God in man and God's saving intent in human life. It is the Christian faith that every moment throughout life God extends the offer of dialogue. Because of our apparent preference for separation, relation to God usually appears to be a threat. Therefore, his invitation usually comes as a challenge to growth and maturity, simultaneously so attractive and so threatening that it may often be called "crisis," so continuous that it may be likened to "growth." Because of the combined pressures of physical change and God's continuous address, at every moment in life a person may go forward in faith, evade in uncertainty, or withdraw in unbelief.

Infancy, childhood, and adolescence form an extended period of development, discovery, and adventure. It is inclined forward; while it is at every moment worthwhile in itself and therefore full of sheer action, it is also pervaded by a sense of preparation, a feeling of expectation, and an unending series of tasks assigned by the older and more mature people in the world. It is also a period of adjustments to changes dictated by the inescapable facts of physiological development, no less demanding and complex in the early physical changes of infancy than in the later sexual changes of adolescence. For all these reasons—and many more—the first twenty-five years of life are said to be a period of individuation, a discovery of self-hood: in infancy, in relation to other persons and things; in early childhood, in relation to like and unlike persons; in middle and later childhood, in relation to same-age persons and other-age persons with authority; in adolescence, in relation to the capacity for individual thought and responsibility.

During infancy, the child is especially at the mercy of other persons, and his response to them is chiefly due to whether they have invited him, puzzled him, or repelled him. In this period, therefore, it is the attitude of other persons that exposes the child to the address of God, and he tends to move forward, evade or withdraw in precisely the same way he is learning to respond to human beings. Even in later years, his response to God as well as to persons will be grounded in the address others have made to him in his infancy, to be reinforced, clarified, or changed as he then can, sometimes at the price of a great struggle for reorientation.

In childhood, individuality is discovered while under the direction of others, a dialectical situation. Individuality is therefore a hard lesson to learn, and the difficulty exposes him to an objective kind of otherness: physical changes, the independent life of parents and teachers, skills to be learned, the wonder and size of the physical environment. Ordinarily, the child will relate to God in terms of his own developing individuality. He may withdraw to infancy and identify God with himself in a dependent *we-feeling;* he may evade and identify God with nature and its objective otherness; he may

43

move forward and identify God as a *you,* a "father," or an "old man." In any event, learning the difficult lesson of identity exposes him along its course to the address of God.

At the peak of childhood there sometimes comes a plateau when the learning tasks of childhood seem to be accomplished and the child seems a small adult in his poise and balance; sometimes childhood plunges directly into the turmoil of adolescence prompted by the cataclysmic physical changes of puberty and the tension of a delayed sexual adulthood. Adolescence, however entered, is a period of desire for immediate independence and the painful accomplishment of intermediate steps, the chief of which, perhaps, is the achievement of some sort of working balance between reason and emotion, and the final goal of which is the achievement of mutuality. Now, mutuality is not possible without individuality; it is the dialogical relationship in which individuality is caught up and fulfilled—not surrendered—in dynamic and productive relationship to other individuals. It is the supreme task of adolescence to discover it; it is a lifelong task to enter into it in some parts and times. It has long been recognized that the adolescent is especially exposed to religious experience. If the tension of individuality-and-mutuality is too much of an adventure, the adolescent may withdraw into a childhood nature worship or an infant we-feeling about God. The adolescent may evade the thrust forward and settle for an emotional rebellion against religious institutions or an intellectual atheism that flaunts the independence of reason. Or, the adolescent may move forward, responding wondrously and openly to the reality of God. The teacher may enter into any of these changing relationships as enabler and guide.

Adulthood is an extended period of time in which the human person, relatively well equipped with individuality, discipline, knowledge, and skills, may deal with the continuous and active presence of God in the world and in life.

The adventure of self-direction characterizes young adulthood. Education either becomes self-directed or grinds to a halt. Jobs must be found and chosen, a vocation discovered. A mate is to be decided upon and a home begun. There are children to decide upon, prepare for, and nurture. Busy, abounding in energy, harassed, leaping forward or swamped with mistakes, the young adult is peculiarly exposed to the address of God. He needs help to see that his life and needs supply the materials for building meaning and purpose.

The achievement of patterns characterizes middle adulthood. If he survives the heart-attack decade, the incessant pressure to keep the income rising to take care of the growing family, to take his place in the community, to exercise his growing fund of knowledge and observation, take their toll of the adult's energy. Old judgments tend to decide new problems. He tends to resist the address of God as disturbing familiar patterns, but he is also peculiarly exposed to unanticipated insight and possibilities. He needs to be surprised by the joy that can come from giving solid form and substance to the divine-human dialogue.

The simplification of life characterizes senior adulthood. The results of his earlier choices begin to show for all to know, he lives with them now because others do, and there is less pressure to make or change a public image. Friends pass away, the younger generation moves away. There is more time and need for thought and memory. Absence and death become living companions. The predominance of material things passes and he becomes especially exposed to spiritual things but he may resist them as signals of debilitation of energy and the shortness of time. He needs the opportunity to serve and be served; he needs help in finding the assurance that dialogue is abiding and real.

Thus, at every age—indeed, at every moment of life from the womb to the tomb—the relationships of life are changing, and the human being is exposed by them to the reality and nearness of God.

He may respond to the invitation of God in faith; when he does so life will be creative, risking—an adventure. He may respond by withdrawing in unbelief; when he does, life will be a search for anonymity, for somebody to give orders—a tragedy. He may respond by evading; when he does, life may seem troublesome, threatening —a rat race. The teacher needs to sense, from the pupil's side of life, where he lives in relation to the invitation of God, and to realize that every level constantly exposes the living human person to the dialogue.

* * *

A person is a learning being.

The complex and constantly changing relationships which the human person sustains inevitably force changes upon him. Human beings have the capacity, in one degree or another, to fit these forces and changes into patterns and to take advantage of them. Persons are therefore not merely the products of these forces, but in some degree their master. These patterns of adjustments have been reduced by educational philosophers and experimentalists to "the laws of learning." These generalizations have been helpful in describing the processes of learning, and have also pointed to a fact, a fallacy, and a challenge. The fact is this: learning is ultimately a mystery rather than a formula. The fallacy is: the only "law," where pupils are concerned, is that every person is different. The challenge is this: Christian educators must develop some appreciation of the special nature of spiritual learning, a phenomenon which cannot be investigated by observing rats in a maze or by analyzing the mastery of typing skills.

Learning begins with *a miracle of readiness*. The so-called law of readiness observes that "when one is ready to act in a certain way, to do so is satisfying; not to do so is annoying." Obviously, one is most ready for dinner when one is hungry. John Dewey's principle in education is that one is most ready to learn when there is a "felt need," a problem to be solved, an interruption of life's normal flow. Paul Tillich's method of correlation makes use of the same principle: Christianity is an answer to each of life's ultimate concerns, and it is the task of the theologian to indicate the correlation. Pupils have deeply seated needs for answers; it is the responsibility of the teacher to listen for the questions actually asked. The need for dialogue is embedded in the human situation; the teacher's task is to find the act or word of initiation to match the response the learner is ready to give. Readiness is a miracle on which both learning and teaching are dependent. On the other hand, it is not enough for the teacher to wait for readiness: in the learning of Christianity, *purpose* may be aroused by touching the wellsprings of life from the pupil's side. Readiness, and learning, too, will follow.

Learning involves *the principle of effort*. The law of exercise (or of use and disuse) is this: "Repeated response to some situation makes repetition easier; disuse makes repetition more difficult." There are three principles involved in this law: recency, frequency, and intensity; given these qualities at their optimum, learning will result. But, of course, practice does not always make perfect, and, besides, religion is not simply a matter of habit-learning or rote memorization, and the success of Loyola's rigorous *Exercises* in the spiritual life is probably due more to the exercise of sheer desire than repetition. The possibility of dialogue is so built into the human situation that it is almost impossible to survive without entering repeatedly into dialogue at some level, and this exercise should serve to make the leap of faith into divine-human relation more trustworthy; perhaps all the teacher needs to do is to point this out in some concrete way. In spiritual learning, the principle of effort is two-sided, for it also enters into the teacher's invitation to dialogue, his crossing over to the pupil's side—an effort so sustained and sympathetic by nature as to justify the radical description, "suffering."

Dissatisfaction is a significant element of spiritual learning. The principle is called "the law of effect": "satisfaction tends to increase learning; dissatisfaction tends to decrease learning." In the spiritual life, the address by God to the individual person is so deeply embedded in human existence that refusal to answer creates a profound discontent. This divinely implanted discontent is, perhaps, one of the strongest incentives to response that man knows about. "Thou hast made us for Thyself," said Augustine in his famous prayer, "and the heart of man is restless until it finds its rest in Thee." This instinctive dissatisfaction with the finite and imperfect, because man has an intimation of the infinite and perfect, forms the basis for the now discredited medieval proof for the existence of God called the ontological argument: it was wholly unnecessary as a "proof" of God's reality, but it grows out of a universal experience that lies at the root of spiritual learning.

The need for meaning is a source of spiritual learning. The law of association rules that learning always proceeds from the known to the unknown. In spiritual knowledge, the reverse is true. The knowledge of God always goes awry—the history of doctrine provides ample evidence—when known models and experiences are used to limit the activity and nature of God. Revelation proceeds from the unknown into the known, and is related by the knower to what is known. Spiritual learning is not so much discernment as disclosure. It has been repeatedly said that man's modern sickness is due to his loss of meaning; that loss was due, in the spiritual field, to his determination to construct it all for himself. In this situation what is needed most is the teaching of awareness; the awareness of need for meaning in response to an invitation already addressed to man.

The desire for expression is always an assistance to spiritual learning. With it the search for principles of spiritual learning has passed beyond the formal laws of learning, but not beyond the common-sense wisdom of teachers in the classroom. How many teachers have insisted to the stammering pupil, "If you do know it, you can say it!" There the implication was that verbalization represented mastery of an idea or fact. In spiritual learning there is a different implication: the Word comes alive when put through the experience of the person into expression—in words, poetry, dance, painting, worship, service. Pupils need to be helped to find a special vocabulary for materializing in tactile form their response to the special Christian content. The Word will be learned in the expressing.

Personal and social influence are factors in spiritual learning. The teacher is inseparable from the lesson. "The Gospel bears the finger-prints of those who pass it on," observed George Albert Coe, and Horace Bushnell said that "the most effective edition of the Gospel is bound in human hide." This principle explains, of course, the effectiveness of Jesus as teacher: he was his message. It explains why the home has more influence on the spiritual development of the child than the church school—for better or for worse. The pupil will always learn most from the teacher he knows and loves. This principle comes to the teacher as both a clue and a caution. His address to the learner may fail to be knowledgeable or brilliant or persuasive, but it must not fail to be genuine. In view of this principle, the best thing for the teacher to do is to offer dialogue with the same One with whom he seeks relation, rather than merely with himself.

*

Every good teacher is a student of students. After all, if he is to venture to cross over to the student's side of experience, he should have some idea of where he is going, and how to get there.

5

Teachers

Teachers are enablers in the search for dialogue.

The Greeks suspected that their great teachers were especially kin to the gods. Socrates, Plato, and Aristotle claimed to be following the dictates of divine reason, and their teaching enabled students to create a way of life guided by the mind more than by passion. The Hebrews respected their teachers as representing Yahweh.

Amos, Jeremiah, and Hosea claimed to be speaking the words of God's judgment, and their prophesying enabled the chosen people to walk more nearly according to the ways and ordinances of the Lord. Jesus was not only called Teacher by his disciples, but Lord as well. Matthew, Peter, and John said that he was the salvation he taught, and his life and sayings enabled his students to catch a vision of grace and to commit acts of love.

The teacher of Christianity is certainly no descendant of the Greek gods, for they kidnapped those they loved. He probably does not feel that he is a mouthpiece of divine judgment, for modern people are painfully diffident about claiming that they have said anything important, to say nothing of prefacing their words with "thus saith the Lord." He does not think of himself as a little Christ, for he knows all too well the uncrossable chasm that exists between his vision of love and his own loving.

He is a person, like the learners, "needing and seeking dialogue," "a center of constantly changing relationships," "a learning being." By what right, then, is he here, in this classroom, with these eyes seeking or avoiding his, these questions of meaning and purpose singing out to him? Certainly the demand is not that he provide or be the answer for them—and that is all right, because no man can do that for another.

The teacher of Christianity is an enabler—a catalyst, an assistant. He is one element for the learners in a life full of inclinations toward fulfillment, one single existence in the midst of all the tremendous inrush of reality on the pupil, and that is all he needs to be—one element, a single existence. He is also an enabler because he is aware of being the only person there who consciously desires to see this throbbing response to existence fulfilled. For the moment, he alone recognizes that for the creative response to occur, a visible and viable initiative must be offered. It is his task to offer, through a challenging of indifference, a crossing over to the other side, a knowledge of the content of study. He cannot create, but he can expose himself to the creative spirit.

So there they are—the beautiful and the misshapen, the quiet and the noisy, the somnolent and the insolent: waiting! He must certainly address them with more than a beatific or hopeful smile; it would obviously be inane to say, "Good morning, and are we all ready for creative dialogue today?" He must be prepared.

*

The teacher of Christianity must be prepared to like pupils.

Considering the many barriers modern man has worked into his social structures and customs to keep people from ever meeting one another, liking one's pupils may require some doing. It is not that the teacher has any reason to dislike them. It is simply that, in the ordinary rounds of life, he would have no reason ever to see them outside of class. This would clearly be true if the church were in the inner city, but it can be equally so in suburbia, where a wave at the shopping center parking lot or an exchange of small talk at a cocktail party is about as close as people ever approach one another. And the chance of meeting would be especially slim if the learners were of a different age-group from that of the teacher, as they often are. The life of contemporary society makes it difficult to know anybody well enough to like him. So, the teacher must be prepared to take the trouble to know his pupils. Much of this effort must take place outside of class sessions, though an alert teacher can learn a great deal about pupils during the teaching-and-learning period and in the few informal moments at his disposal before and after. One great teacher has said that "a teacher should know his pupils well enough to play with them."

A teacher should know his pupils as different from himself. He needs to know the extent and ground of those chasms of age, experience, and knowledge that make instruction possible. This suggests that he will need to know all that the address, phone number, and birth date will tell him, and much more: school life, reading interests, vocational skills, hobbies, the relationships of home, and so on and on. These bare facts, when brooded over and put together, may suddenly add up to an insight into the wondrous and fragile individuality of the pupil as a human person.

A teacher should also know his pupils as like himself. Whatever superficial and helpful similarities of class, habits, and experiences there may be between them, it is important also to cast the sounding line down deep until it comes to rest on the universal fears and joys of human existence. This is the level at which initiative and response may sometimes meet in a translucent moment of dialogue, when teacher and pupil stand together on similar ground facing the divine.

A teacher should know his pupils in groups as well as singly. It is one thing to know and like a ten-year-old boy; it may be quite another thing to know and like fifteen of them for an hour in the strangely shaped room behind the organ on Sunday morning. The boy whom one knows to be a rebellious lad at home may be a well-mannered gentleman among his peers. The harassed mother who is constantly asking perplexing questions about child psychology may present another sort of problem in a class on the Flight from Egypt. A man who enjoys the company of individual executives may find a dozen of them together a terrifying experience. Teaching involves an individual relation within a group relation, and the teacher should be prepared for it.

If the teacher actually prepares to know his pupils in all these ways, the chances are that he will be prepared to like them. At least he will know them well enough to know what his problems are.

*   *

The teacher of Christianity should be prepared to like the content. A teacher who has no particular interest in the subject matter he is teaching is a pathetic creature, like the sorry violinist who detests music, or the airplane pilot who is afraid of heights. The content of Christianity is vast. If the teacher cannot wax enthusiastic about its history, perhaps its philosophy will excite him. If this is the situation, he should be honest enough to see that changes are made before he begins. Somewhere in the range of fields which comprise the subject matter of Christianity, there is a subject in which his interests will fit. Learners have a way of knowing when their teacher is bored or feigning interest. It is a capacity not worth tempting.

Liking a subject implies that one will be prepared to work at it. One will read everything he can lay his hands on that bears on it; indeed, everything he reads will seem to have some relation to it. He will gather information from every quarter—experts, lectures, secondhand bookshops. He will find illustrations at every turn— in newspapers, daily events, chance conversations. He will mull over his accumulating data and find them associating themselves in new and exciting concepts, which must be checked against what others have thought. His interest will become a magnet that will attract the attention of others who will feed information his way. He will learn both the top and the bottom of the subject, and he will want this kind of knowledge, especially if he is teaching it to the young. He will know it and all around it, finding more and more fields which impinge upon his interest and illuminate it. He will someday find it coming out of his ears. Then he knows he is ready to begin teaching it—even if, all this time, he has already been meeting classes on the subject for months.

*　　*　　*

The teacher of Christianity should be prepared to like teaching.

For reasons that may forever remain obscure, the teaching of Christianity in Sunday schools seems to attract people who do not really enjoy the teaching-and-learning process. For reasons that are probably less obscure, they are not relieved of the agony even when it is apparent to everybody within earshot of the classroom. The teacher's voice drones on in grim severity, the interminable pauses while the teacher gropes for another thought are filled with the sounds of incipient pupil insurrection, and when the period of torture is ended the class bursts into the open outside the room with unconcealed relief.

Liking teaching is both demanding and exhilarating. Liking to teach means liking to prepare the lesson—paintakingly, thoroughly, for every possible question and challenge. It involves one in the study of teaching, of the techniques of presentation, of the methods of conducting a class session, of the comparison of teaching experiences. It means believing in the educating process, enjoying the give and take. It means planning how all these elements may fit together in regard to the particular lesson to come. And it means, at last, with all this preparation behind one, coming into the classroom eager for the fray.

*   *   *   *

The teacher of Christianity should be prepared to develop and exercise his special talents.

Every aptitude and interest of the teacher should be placed at the disposal of the class session. What he is fortunate enough to possess, he will need to develop and use. Every teacher has some special capacities, and some are required of every teacher.

A good memory is an invaluable asset in a classroom: the teacher who cannot remember an important date in a history lesson is as ineffective and amusing as the automobile mechanic who has misplaced his 11/16th inch off-center ratchet-drive socket wrench at precisely the moment he has the oil pan ready to come off. The teacher who can remember and quote the question Johnny asked three weeks ago, now that it is relevant, is a good teacher. If a teacher thinks he does not have a good memory, he should do everything in his power to develop it; if he thinks he has a good one, he should practice filling it to its absolute capacity.

Humor is a universal gift, and it can be developed. Of the two kinds, the capacity to tell a joke and the capacity to recognize one, the latter may be the more important in the classroom. And of two other kinds, the capacity to laugh at oneself and the capacity to laugh at someone else, the former is the more important. In any case, the learning that is accomplished in a good laugh after twenty minutes of serious concentration is probably more than that accomplished in fifty minutes without one.

Honesty is an indispensable talent for the teacher of Christianity. Determination is significant, patience is effective, kindness is essential; each may be nurtured, and the combination of them literally makes a good teacher.

Whatever his talents are—ten, or five, or one—the teacher of Christianity should be prepared to identify them objectively and deepen them prodigiously—for the sake of his pupils and the lesson.

*   *   *   *   *

The teacher of Christianity must be prepared to love God in the classroom.

It is not necessary that the teacher be a saint, but it is required of the teacher that he not ask his students to go where he is unwilling to go. Specifically, he must be prepared not only to seek out God in the secrecy of his closet but also in the presence of the class. He must be willing to speak of his understanding of God honestly, whether it be vague or clear. He should be willing to share his faith and his doubts. He must be prepared to admit that he is, himself, engaged in the quest. He is called upon to make his offer of dialogue under the comparatively public gaze of the class.

*

Teachers of Christianity are persons who are prepared to offer dialogue, as effectively as they can, to learners. As they do, they become enablers in the common search and participators in divine grace.

6

Content

Content is the objective element in dialogue.

In Christianity, the special, subjective content—the life of dialogue —and the ordinary, objective content—the facts about dialogue— interpenetrate. However, there has not generally been much real confusion between the special, active, self-communicating content, and the ordinary, factual, traditional content.

From time to time, it is true, it has been the tendency of an age to separate them and give excessive attention to the factual content. The period of medieval scholasticism in the fourteenth and fifteenth centuries, and of Protestant scholasticism in the late sixteenth century, are examples; so, too, was the Age of Reason in the eighteenth century. In the twentieth century, the tendency is to reduce the content of Christianity to a scientific account of institutions, doctrines, and language. History should teach how threatening the earlier dissociations of the factual content of Christianity have been to spiritual life and warn contemporary Christians of the dangers implicit in the present trend.

In general, however, two principles have been simultaneously maintained which have served to keep the spiritual life of Christians anchored to objective facts, and the facts of Christianity spiritually alive. The first is the characteristic conviction that in the Christian life the most highly sophisticated of the scholars has no necessary advantage over the most unlettered of the saints. The second is the consistent assumption that an informed and learned Christian is a more effective Christian than an uninformed Christian. Indeed, the most memorable and celebrated Christians have, themselves, been both: Paul, Augustine, Luther, Jonathan Edwards, and Albert Schweitzer, for example.

Alfred N. Whitehead, borrowing from a medieval mystic, observed that education should involve an exposure to greatness. During its long history, Christianity, together with Judaism before it, has concreted a vast fund of greatness—acts and ideas precipitated by the divine-human dialogue in which Christianity specializes. The objective content of Christianity offers an encounter with all the greatness the life of man can encompass—the apostles, martyrs, and builders: they conquered kingdoms, enforced justice, received promises; they escaped the edge of the sword, won strength out of weakness, put foreign armies to flight; they suffered mocking and scourging and even chains and imprisonment; they were stoned, they were killed with the sword; they were destitute, afflicted, ill-treated. They were sinners and they were made whole. It also offers an exposure to all the greatness the human mind can bear: the notion of a chosen people and a sacred history; the thought of God penetrating human life in Jesus of Nazareth; the intricacies of trinitarian controversies and doctrine; the principle of justification by faith; the vision of a universal kingdom of love and peace; the self-revelation of God.

The objective content of Christianity is a tradition and a stance pulsating with God's acts and man's responses. The tragedy—the sin—of the ordinary teaching of Christianity is that it veils the greatness by cutting it up into bits of littleness, makes it manageable by making it boring. The teaching of Christianity will never go well until the teacher finds the content of Christianity exciting and great for himself, and until he learns to let the thrill of the objective content reach through to the life of the learners.

*

Leaning upon the work of secular educators, Christian education has habitually divided itself into two streams of thinking about content, the "traditional" and the "progressive."

The traditional school tends to emphasize the materials of study. The content of education, according to it, is contained primarily in the textbook, or the references, or the lecture notes of the teacher. When the textbook is the Bible, it is a particularly difficult point of view to modify. The purpose of the class session is to master these materials, and the craft of teaching consists especially of clarifying, repeating, fixing. The assumption is that the essence of the content will find its own way into the actual thinking and living of the students, and even if it doesn't, it has been worth the transmission in the classroom.

In contrast, the progressive school emphasizes the materials of life. The content, according to it, is primarily to be found in the events of the school and the classroom, the interests of the learners, and the attitudes of the teacher. The purpose of the class session is to focus all these fluid qualities upon some problem and work through to its solution. The theory is that facts and information will emerge and organize themselves around successful problem-solving experiences, and even if they don't, the period in the classroom has been a good experience.

In general, it is possible to say that the two schools are lined up against and for John Dewey, respectively. Denominational curriculum materials have attempted to follow one or the other principle, and, more recently, to attempt some sort of compromise in the hope of securing the obvious advantages of both. The difficulty, it would seem, is that the two leading theories of curriculum have derived from the teaching of nonreligious content—reading, writing, and arithmetic—rather than from teaching the distinctive nature of the Christian content. From the point of view of the teaching of Christianity as the art of enabling dialogue, the secular distinctions would seem to diminish in importance. The special content of Christianity —the self-revelation of God to man and man's response—precipitates the objective content of Christianity—the acts of God and the responsive activities of man. The one produces the other, and the other illuminates the one.

*   *

There is a living relationship between "the life of dialogue" and "the facts of dialogue." The content of Christianity is the link between, holding teaching-and-learning together.

In the teaching of Christianity, content is a means to an end, and of the same stuff as the end. In some subjects, the situation is quite different. Learning the skills of drawing is a means to the goal of architecture, but fine architecture is not the same as skilled drawing. It is sometimes argued that the thought processes learned in mastering the mechanics of the Latin language will help the dogged student someday solve mathematical problems. It was said of Mr. Dooley's infamous school that "it didn't matter much what the student was learning so long as he didn't like it." The case with the teaching of Christianity is not like that. The content is the same as the goal; the means and the end are not qualitatively distinct. The facts are inseparably related to the life.

In the teaching of Christianity, the content deals with life, but not haphazardly, at the mercy of capricious interests and chance events, as was often the case with progressive education. Whatever the individual and ingenious responses of man to God's address in different times and situations, God is always the same in nature and intent. From across the vast spectrum of man's history, every response focuses on the single stimulus, and the innumerable insights are reflections from a single gem. The content of Christianity is thus both living and unified.

The teaching-and-learning of Christianity deals with content, but not mechanically. Since the content is itself not rigid, it is difficult to treat it rigidly. The content is as living as the breathing and thinking of those who created it. It is the task of the teacher to permit the life to flame up again by direct contact, for the dialogue of history is not unlike the present dialogue of the students, and the differences in time and place only make content less mechanical.

The content of Christianity is a unity of life and fact, of objective and subjective. The teacher cannot be content to separate them, even though he must identify the separate strands in order that the learners may feel their interplay and identify the same strands in their own living as they constantly tend toward the miracle of unity.

In the teaching of the Christian content, materials and methods must be mutually appropriate. There may be justification in the teaching of mathematics, for example, for holding the child to interminable repetition so that he can catch a glimpse of logarithmic functions. It may be appropriate in the English public school for the tutor to hold up the cocksure boy to the scorn of the class, as a fallacy in the interpretation of a line of Chaucer is revealed. But one cannot teach love by hating, and in the teaching of Christianity the content is love, the material is love, and the method is love. When God needed to teach his ultimate lesson, he sent his Son; theologians have been struggling ever since to explain how the material and method, means and end of the Incarnation, were the same.

*   *   *

Ordinarily, the teacher of Christianity is provided with "curriculum materials." During the last twenty-five years, spectacular achievements have been made by denominational organizations in the improvement and production of texts and guides. Many of them are very helpful. Some of them are too helpful: they are so complete that they intimidate and dominate the teacher. Whatever the materials he may have at hand, from a handsomely illustrated modern textbook to a tattered copy of the Scriptures, the teacher must constantly build the actual curriculum step by step, insight by insight, breath by breath.

The content must be brought into contact with the local situation. It is impossible for a writer in Central City or an editor in Denominational Towers to know the lives, problems, interests, and events of this class this week. That is the teacher's responsibility. Bringing that material into contact with these lives will require taking some liberties with any prepared guide. Only the teacher can make the content relevant, and he can accomplish this only at the price of constant diligence and imagination.

The teacher should permit the learners to have a share in developing the content. The "unwritten" or "hidden" agenda the learners bring with them from their own lives and experiences should have a great deal to do with determining the agenda of the course. The teacher cannot merely guess at this unseen content: he must ask for it in ways that will actually bring it forth, and then, having exposed himself, he must be honest and informed enough to be able to order the objective content in terms of their subjective content.

The content must be balanced and complete. If the teacher is flexible enough to make the material relevant, he must be disciplined and informed enough to make the material eventually broad and synoptic. There may be one learner who is moved by the parable of the prodigal son, and another who will be set aflame by the parable of the dishonest steward which immediately follows.

Every separate unit of study is to be set in the context of the Christian dialogue as a whole. This dialogue is not only in the present local church, but also in the contact of the community of dialogue with the world at large, and in the events of history and Scripture as well. It includes those who have been notably responsive to the address of God and those who are still timid, those who seem to live an ordered life of response and those for whom response is an occasional and cataclysmic earthquake. The part is in the whole, and both the whole and the parts are greater than any group of learners and any separate item of content.

*

It is the intent of the teacher that the content of Christianity will not merely be another item added to the subjects the learner deals with in the course of his daily life, but will pervade and penetrate them all. The content of Christianity is thus not taught and learned merely in the classroom during the class session. There will be study by the learners and the teacher outside the class. The content of the class will be related to their conscious acts of service and sharing. It will become part of their worshiping. It will be reinforced and illustrated in leisure-time activities, on the job, in the home. The content is the objective element that, permeating the life of man, sustains and enables its fulfillment in dialogue.

7

Environment

The environment is the context of dialogue.

    Dialogue is a mystery, but it is not a disembodied mystery like the ghost of Hamlet's father or the abstract ideas of Plato. It is one of the characteristics of Christianity that it takes time, place, and situation seriously. The Prologue to the Johannine Gospel defines the incarnation as the concretion of the eternal Word, which was with God and was God in the beginning, into flesh, where it dwelt among us, so that we could see and know the glory of God. Luke makes it clear that it happened in the days of Caesar Augustus, Quirinius, and Herod; Matthew that it occurred in Bethlehem of Judea.

The essence of the doctrine of Incarnation is that the divine and the human can and do interpenetrate in such a way that the divine intent and the salvation of man are accomplished without destroying the uniqueness of God or the independence of man. The Judaic-Christian understanding of creation applies the same sort of principle: the personal brings the nonpersonal into orderly and objective material being, and then penetrates the material world in such a way as to produce the sentient and self-directed life of man. Dialogue is, also, an embodied mystery: it is the discovery and celebration of a spiritual unity between God and man in the midst of man's material life. The context does not alter the address of God, but it does affect the ways and forms of man's responses. Dialogue always occurs to this here-and-now man, in terms of that there-and-then situation.

The mysterious light and voice stopped Saul of Tarsus in his tracks on the road to Damascus, whence he was bent on pursuing the persecution of the Christians. The voice Augustine heard was that of a child playing in a neighboring garden, while he was wrestling with the claims of Christianity as a revealed religion over those of Manichaeism as an electric philosophy. The insight that the just are saved by faith alone came to Martin Luther as he was preparing a course of lectures on the Epistle to the Galatians in the drafty tower room of his quarters in Wittenberg.

Johnny and Mary and Teacher, the problems of yesterday and the void after a hurried breakfast and the plans for this evening, the movie last night and balancing the checkbook and the Christmas

67

pageant, the summer's vacation and a walk in the snow and a flat tire on the way to work, the stars and the trees and the temperature are all realities that are readying for the moment of dialogue and determine its unique form.

The environment will not make or break the teaching-and-learning relationship, but it is either an ally or an obstacle. The teacher will, therefore, be sensitive to the setting of learning and do what he can to make it a friend rather than an enemy.

*

The personal environment of dialogue is the fellowship of seeking and responding that has bound Christians together for centuries. It was produced in the uncertain years following the death and return of Christ as a personal response of loyalty to him. The early band of followers gathered together, providing for one another, sharing what they had, remembering Jesus' words and acts, in an interim of waiting and expecting. *Sharing* and *expecting* created the *fellowship*. It was crystallized and vitalized when it became clear that the message of the incarnation was to be kept alive and shared with the rest of the world. The apostles began to tell the story of the birth and life, the passion and resurrection of the Son of God. They repeated his doings and expanded his teachings. *Kerygma* and *didache* created the *koinonia*. It was strengthened and completed when it became necessary to stand against a world culture of competing philosophies and an empire of idolatrous ambitions. The early Christians sought, when it was possible, to present a rational and convincing account of the mysteries of God's acts to the non-Christian minds of the world. At other times, it became necessary to tighten the organization and purify the faith in the face of persecution and death. *Theology* and *martyrdom* created the *church*.

The history of Christianity bears witness that these three creative processes have never ceased working. Roland Bainton points out that if we could just find the right forty persons, we could know a man who knew a man who knew a man . . . who knew Jesus. They, and innumerable others like them, have keep the *fellowship,* the *koinonia,* and the *church* alive—a contiguous body of those who have responded in some fashion, to some degree, with some consciousness, to the address of God.

A remnant of this reality is to be found in hectic potluck suppers with crying babies and too many beans and pies for a balanced meal, in swaying teen-agers in crossed-hand circles around dying campfires, and in gatherings of spectators on Sunday mornings for indifferent singing and absentminded listening. But even there, from time to time when occasion demands, and certainly in some of the things of a more conscious nature that churches do—a daring support of a drive for racial equality, a night ministry to alcoholics, a student conference of intense concentration—there is evident an island of concern and love in a surrounding sea of competition, distance, and alienation.

The cloud of witnesses, struggling and sinning, tripping and triumphing, is in some sense present as one reaches for dialogue, making more clear by their responses what the address of God may be like, supporting by their trials and victories the timid faith of the current questor. The doctrine of the Communion of Saints, which usually seems quaint and otherworldly, is one way of describing this dynamic content of dialogue. A community of worship, work, and study is an invaluable aid to the teacher of Christianity, and that is what the local church should be.

*   *

The physical environment also affects the search. An appreciative and sensitive relation to surroundings is always a positive assistance to personal dialogue. A beautiful room cannot make learning successful, but it can help. It is incredible what physical obstacles to the teaching-and-learning process churches can sometimes provide behind the sign "Third Grade Classroom." Dingy, dark, and dank cubicles, occupied by human spirits but one hour a week, and crowded with a table too large and with too many chairs, are frequent fare. Now and then a church provides a functional new formica-and-glass fashion piece straight out of the public school architect's copybook, except that, since it is used so little, it has a distinctly anti-human and antiseptic air about it. It might be a great deal better to meet under the trees.

A more conducive setting for dialogue would be a place that looked and felt something more like a "family room," not the formal notion of a sitting room where people perch uncomfortably on chairs and try to make the time pass with small talk, but a room for living: for sitting on the floor, listening to music, making things, looking up answers, arguing and talking and playing. If the room is, itself, a miserable affair, there may be a great deal the teacher and the class can do about color and light and heat and ventilation. Some essential learning may occur in the process. No teacher, sensitive to the needs of his learners and the beauty of the world about him, will be content to meet in a room that drives people apart and sets them against one another.

But decoration, alone, is not enough. One can tell, when one enters a science laboratory, what it is that is taught-and-learned there. Everything in the room has a functional purpose. The same should be true of the setting for dialogue, and the serious teacher will work at the room until it begins to speak, in small if not massive ways, of what it is hoped will happen there. If his particular approach is thought and conversation, the room's equipment will invite people to meditate and talk. If study of content is the plan, there will be books and places to read, maps and charts and pictures. If mature group research is the strategy, the room will be set for a seminar: a table with space for papers and writing, and reference materials at hand. If the class is for children, it may be necessary for the session to be able to shift from one activity to another, perhaps even in the same room.

And, since a vertical dimension is the essence of dialogue, the place will somehow, but unmistakably, reflect this reference. Some classrooms suggest the assumption that a single faded and dusty picture of a sickly Jesus is all that is necessary. Others have built into them folding worship centers which can be tucked out of the way when the class is engaged in something other than singing hymns and taking up the collection. It may be necessary to discover some other symbols. It should be expected that the room reveal that it is a temporary container for the quest after dialogue, through an objective content, and in the context of the historic community of seekers.

There is good reason, also, for taking the quest outside the room. If access to the world beyond can be built into the room, the movement can be made so much the easier and more natural. On a spring morning, the right spot may be a patch of lawn under an oak tree. In midsummer, it may be a shady flight of steps. When studying the history of worship, it may be the chancel or the organ loft. The alert teacher will note these spots and be ready to move to them; it may even be possible, through tactful gardening and the adjustment of unused spaces, to create some of these supplementary settings for dialogue.

*　　*　　*

There are individual people in every community who would never be on the staff of the church school, or consider themselves teachers of Christianity, who would be invaluable resources on special subjects: medical people with their knowledge of human illness, psychiatrists with their insights into human problems, historians with their special information about men and movements, scientists

71

with their facts about the world and the universe, artists with their creative awareness of the world, businessmen with their knowledge of people, laborers with their sensitivity to the attitudes of the exploited. Each human being is a specialist in the life of man. They are all part of the dialogue. The alert teacher may actually introduce them into the teaching-and-learning process.

*

The teaching-and-learning of Christianity takes place in relation to the total environment of the learners. It is not all simply positive. The teacher will do what he can to be sensitive to what the environment is saying. He will turn it toward the support of dialogue when he can. He will make use of it, whatever its moods, to keep the developing spiritual life of his learners firmly rooted in time and space.

8

Lesson Plans

A lesson plan is a design for enabling dialogue.

Design is an essential element of any artist's work, and it is of the teaching art, as well. The importance of preparing a plan for a class session has been universally recognized in teacher's colleges and educational institutes. Unfortunately, the rigor and thoroughness with which they have traditionally enforced the discipline of planning on fledgling teachers have tended to turn a creative art into a dreaded drudgery. The fact remains, however, that good class sessions, like great symphonies, seldom result from lack of design.

Of course, mystery cannot be made to appear upon command, and dialogue cannot be materialized at the wave of a lesson plan, no matter how well thought out it may be. The address of God is prior to man's acts, and therefore cannot be manipulated. Experience has demonstrated that magical incantations, tribal dances, and burnt sacrifices do not influence God's acts. Spiritual reality cannot be precipitated in experience, as can ferrous sulphate by adding ferrous oxide to sulphuric acid. Military victories cannot be guaranteed by brilliant battle plans. Dialogue does not come by design, alone. Dialogue is free, like the Spirit that "bloweth where it listeth."

What is being sought by the teacher of Chistianity is fulfillment of the incomplete nature of man, a response to the inrush of reality upon the isolated soul, a leap into the uncertain adventure of existence. It is a sacred task to participate in the moment of another's becoming. To stand beside the learner in it is to stand upon holy ground. To act as enabler there is worth the teacher's best. Being wholly present and available to the learner requires of the teacher, dissociated and diffused as man's powers tend always to be, a continuous readying of experience and knowledge. The teacher of Christianity will constantly be learning about his pupils, mastering the content, evaluating and disciplining his own native gifts, improving the environment of learning. The time comes, however, when that certain course or this specific session requires direct planning.

Making lesson plans is the transition between thinking about teaching and actually teaching a lesson. It ought to be as exciting as the actual class session.

*

The planning of an entire course is something like preparing to create a painting. It is essentially an artistic experience. It begins with contemplation, gathering and reviewing resources, combing the ideas of others, mulling upon one's own inner resources and conflicts. The process may be extended or brief: sometimes the whole pattern will appear immediately, sometimes it comes during conscious application to the subject, sometimes it comes only as the result of painful and dogged pursuit of elusive principles and wearying details. It is a period always marked by preoccupation and concentration. And then—the design is "there," immediately recognizable, including all the relevant parts and excluding the unnecessary.

The design of a course will eventually include an outline of the material to be covered by the learners. Sometimes it will have great detail, sometimes it will have in it huge holes to be filled in later by the dint of hard digging, sometimes it will be "right" from the beginning and remain practically unchanged as the course proceeds. Usually, it is refined and perfected in session-by-session preparation. It will be selective: no workable design includes everything, and it is always distinguished by the care with which it omits. It will, of course, be constructed in terms of the specific learners for whom the course is offered. Whether it be a topic outline or a sentence outline, it is the working pattern for the course, and is to be tested by constant use of its inherent structure.

The design will also provide a time schedule. This involves a matching of natural divisions in the outline with the number and length of sessions available. Sometimes there will be an easy and obvious matching of the components, but sometimes the two parts will seem to have nothing in common, and arbitrary decisions must be made in advance and held tentatively.

A list of resources is an essential part of the overall design. Books, activities, trips, visitors, specialists, and illustrations will be listed, located for easy reference when needed, perhaps collected for use. Sometimes this list will require a great deal of research, and sometimes much of it will already be at hand. Eventually, this list must be coordinated with the outline of material and the time schedule.

A statement of hoped-for outcomes will be drawn up. It is necessary for the design to be complete, to have some concrete, if tentative, vision of the way in which the material and the events of the course may reinforce and enable the possibilities of dialogue for these particular learners. How does the material help the teacher to cross over to the student's side of experience? What may be the actual function of these ideas, these stories from history, these illustrations of encounter and heroism and failure, in the living of these learners?

It does not matter which of the elements of the design is completed first. Some teachers will think first of goals; others will work more easily in the content first. In any case, the final plan for the course will include all the elements, not in fixed and immutable form, but as a design for enabling dialogue.

*   *

Planning each session is the artistic job of construction. In it the teacher is more craftsman than designer. It involves detail work, the fitting of small bits into the whole plan, the perfecting and changing of parts of the vision. Since the pressure is on to prepare specifically for the coming class session, preparation at this level tends to carry its own motivation. There is also a tendency to think of each unit of work as complete in itself. The total design, however, must never be forgotten. A double rule commands the craft of construction: "each session grows out of the preceding session"; "each session is part of the whole."

The first step, therefore, in the plan for the next session, is to define its relation to the whole design and to the ongoing experience of the learners. The teacher is thus constantly driven to his own review. He is also kept close to the learners' "unwritten agenda" for the course. Events between sessions may determine the teacher to insert an entirely new unit for the next session. Next week, then, he will be driven back to the overall plan with increased responsibility.

Resources must be gathered and selected and used for each session. The list of resources from the overall design will be constantly referred to, but it will need constant enlargement. Some will be selected for the learners' use. If assignments have been made, a place for them must be planned in the coming session.

It is in preparing for specific sessions that the teacher does his most concentrated reading. There is an inviolable rule for teachers at this point, whether their learners be kindergartners or college seniors: get to the original resources. If the subject is biblical, there is nothing to replace the Bible itself, helpful though history and commentary may be. If the material is history, the works and autobiography of the man himself must be searched out and read. And there is a second rule, like unto the first: no matter how many times the teacher has "taught" this subject, this coming session demands new preparation. There is nothing that will put a class to sleep like a sleepy teacher, and a teacher who thinks he already knows his subject is already half asleep.

Some specific plans must be made also for procedure in the class session. Two arbitrary choices are made in advance: a point of departure for the beginning of the session, and a point of arrival for its conclusion. The choice of a beginning will be more arbitrary than the choice of an ending, of course. In between, the session grows as it goes.

The point of departure may be a review of the last session, or of assignments made then, of events that have occurred since the last session, or an entirely new idea. In any case, the teacher is responsible for choosing it in advance as carefully and as wisely as he can, and for beginning with it as decisively and provocatively as possible.

The conclusion may be a summary of what has been covered in this session, the introduction of a new idea beyond what has been arrived at, assignment for use in the next session. In any case, the teacher has chosen it in advance, and keeps it in mind as the session develops; he will not push toward it, and if it is necessary to substitute a different conclusion, he will be in a position to do so consciously.

For the bulk of the session, that huge space between departure and arrival, he will have planned the illustrations and activities and have chosen the methods of presentation to be used. Some days the session may go flawlessly just as he had prepared it; sometimes the session will bear little resemblance to his plan. In either event, he must be ready to respond if invited and well enough prepared to be free to sense the slightest evidences of that hoped-for movement.

* * *

The artist's construction is not finished with the filling of the canvas, and the teacher's lesson plan is not completed with the ringing of the bell at the end of the session. The artistic discipline of criticism is part of the creative act. The best time for the teacher to review the class session and compare it with his lesson plan is immediately after the last learner has left the room. He will develop, in time, the capacity to recall specific comments and reactions from the individual learners and his own handling of details. He may make notes. If the session has gone exactly according to his plan, he must ask whether he missed signals from the class indicating divergent interests and needs. If it departed wildly from his plan, he must question the validity of his plan and his conduct of the session. He will ask himself how this session fits into the whole design of the course, and what clues his answers give him for the next session soon to come. And, most important of all, he must think through again the situation of each learner, asking what has happened of spiritual significance in this time together and what may happen next in the developing individual response to God. He has already begun work on the next lesson plan.

*

Making lesson plans is the transition between thinking about teaching and actually teaching. It is part of an artistic process of contemplation and construction, so crammed with awareness and concentration that it literally bursts into communication, throwing off the covers that hide the expressiveness of experienced things, enabling a viewer to forget himself in the delight of experiencing the world about him for himself. Teaching Christianity is just such a creative act. In the background lie the throbbing ebb and flow of life, the dynamic thrust toward response to an eternal address. There has been, for the teacher, an awareness of the living content of Christianity, the needs of learners and the responsibility to be a participant in the offer of dialogue God makes to all men. There has been a concentration on the materials with which he might work, producing a design for sharing. Communication can be the only possible result of this concentration and construction, a bursting into the open of interest and concern that intercepts the slackness of routine living and reveals the possibilities for the fulfillment of existence that lie at hand, "closer than breathing." The design and preparation should have been fascinating in themselves. Now he must venture forward with faith in the teaching-and-learning process. He may not succeed, of course. Indeed, he may fail miserably. But even if this should not be his moment for the Kingdom, it is at least the moment for which he has prepared, and, after all, the class is about to begin.

9

Lecturing

Lecturing is a method of enabling the teaching-and-learning dialogue in which only one voice is audible.

Everyone knows, of course, what the lecture method is. Most teachers in colleges and universities, and many in high schools use it. Nearly all radio and television commentators employ the same technique. The doctor explaining to the patient what he must do to cooperate with the healing process, the salesman extolling the virtues of his product, the traffic policeman expounding to the guilty driver the rules he has just violated, are all lecturing. Sermons are lectures, and so was the most famous of them all, the Sermon on the Mount.

Lecturing is the method, par excellence, of formal education. The teacher talks, more or less continuously, to the class. The learners listen, take notes, and ponder what the teacher has said, but mostly later and outside the classroom. Sometimes there are a few questions, but these are signals for shorter, more specific lectures. The method is characterized by a steady flow of information going from the teacher to the learners. By its critics, it is sometimes called the "I-tell-and-you-listen" technique; sometimes they say that it is a way of "getting the information from the teacher's notes into the student's notes without passing through the head of either." These criticisms are justified when the lecturer has been inept. The address was, indeed, a monologue, and no communication took place, largely because the teacher's poor performance prevented response from the learners. It is not necessary, however, for the response to be audible for there to be real dialogue. Some of the most effective teaching ever done has been accomplished through lecturing, and everyone who has had any formal education beyond mid high school will remember occasions on which he was stirred to his depths by an accomplished lecturer; his memory of those events will likely include both ideas and facts as well as the deeply felt response.

Lecturing is a valid form of teaching. Every teacher of Christianity will use it, at least some of the time, and many will depend upon it almost exclusively. Because there are both advantages and disadvantages in its use and certain conditions which must be met if it is to be used effectively, every teacher should study the art of lecturing and be prepared to be candid in judging his own capacities for it.

*

Some essential conditions must be met if lecturing is to be an effective method of teaching-and-learning.

The content must be important. This is, of course, one reason that lecturing has been the traditional method in the teaching of the classics: the material has its own attraction to both the teacher and the learners. This has often been used as an argument by teachers of the Bible for relying on the lecture method almost exclusively: the content is worth knowing about. For the same reason, however, lecturing also goes best when the material is factual or demonstrable: most classes in history, mathematics, and science use presentational methods. Again, when the content is vast in scope and the important thing is for the class to glimpse a broad spectrum of connected ideas or interrelated events, the lecture is often the most efficient method of presenting it. The lecture, better than any other form, can cover a wide range of material quickly. Survey courses in college, or the introductory courses at a graduate school, provide good material for lecturing. In the field of Christianity, the surveys of Hebrew history and introductions to Christian doctrines may well be handled as lecture courses. And, finally, when the content is technical to a high degree, and basic information about it is possessed by only one member of the community, the lecture is the obvious choice of method. Many courses in medical schools can only be handled by a specialist lecturer, and in the churches there is often need for lectures on specific problems, for example, in the field of race relations.

The lecture method assumes that the learners are equipped to listen effectively. It is clear that some skills in hearing, taking notes, remembering, and analyzing are necessary. So, also, is the skill of silent participation. Since public schools provide training in these skills, it is not necessary for the church to do so, but it is the course of wisdom to be certain that these skills have been acquired to some degree before utilizing the lecture method extensively with any group of learners in the church. In general, this means that the learners will be at least fifteen years of age, and that the church will use lecturing sparingly before that and wisely after. Readiness is especially important when teaching is to be done chiefly by lecturing, and the teacher of Christianity should be as certain as he can that his learners are already interested in the subject before he elects to handle it exclusively by talking to them about it.

Effective lecturing also assumes that the teacher possesses at least some of the skills of public speaking. The first rule of lecturing is "Speak up!" No lecture is worth the trouble if it cannot be heard. A few notable teachers have been miserable speakers, but most good lecturers, without any question, have been good speakers. At least a minimum of enunciation, volume, vocal quality, and personality are required of the lecturer, and the teacher of Christianity would do well to be very candid with himself about these matters before he opts for lecturing. If he is determined to lecture and is diffident about his capacities, let him get some training!

The teacher must also know the subject about which he is to lecture. Unless he knows more about it than the learners, there is no reason for them to meet, and if they do the lecturer will probably make a fool of himself. No one knows that better than the lecturer who has himself suffered through a course he does not know well enough. The second rule of lecturing is "Bone up!" It is impossible to give a good lecture without preparation.

The successful lecturer is a systematic thinker. The third rule of lecturing is "Outline!" Often the brilliant lecturer has nothing really new to say on the subject; everything he has to present can be read in any one of a dozen textbooks. He communicates the material because he can isolate the parts and understand their relationships and submit these elements to the learners with such clarity that they can grasp and evaluate the points for themselves. Learners turn off their receivers when they are bombarded with a continuous flow of words or a rambling sequence of facts, no matter how skillfully delivered, but they will never tune out when the points march along in clearly defined sequence, even if they are not particularly original.

*　　*

The lecture method of teaching-and-learning has some very great advantages. Efficiency is one: one teacher may instruct at one time any number of pupils that can be brought within the range of his voice and presence. The ultimate development in this direction may be educational television, and some large universities have applied this technique to lecture halls of alarming proportions. Further, a great deal of material may be covered in a short time, and there is practically no equipment needed beyond a place to speak from and a place for listeners to sit and write. The sermon on Sunday morning, together with the high pulpit at the end of a long hall equipped with benches in straight rows, is an example of this sort of efficiency. There may be special as well as regular occasions on which it is desirable for the entire community of Christian learners to be instructed at once in this fashion.

There are advantages, too, in dealing with the content. A fresh or authoritative interpretation of the subject may be given in this way better than in any other. The teacher does the original work, and as an authority lays the outcome before the learners. It is important, in the teaching of Christianity, that learners encounter original scholars of the Christian content, be they homegrown or imported. Further, when one mind handles the material and one voice communicates the results, a precision and clarity is possible that can never come from group discussion, and usually does not come from the individual learner's study. It should also be pointed out to beginning teachers of Christianity that one great advantage of the lecture method is that the lecturer need know only a *little* more than his learners in order to lecture effectively about it. The advantage to him is that he is in control of the material to be dealt with and need never go beyond the point to which he is prepared: he can always say, "That is a good question; I will attempt to deal with it in my next lecture."

* * *

There are also some very great disadvantages built into the lecture method of teaching-and-learning. The first, and perhaps most obvious, has to do with the learner: the whole situation tends to make him a passive receiver; it is almost impossible for the lecturer to know whether there is a real response to what he is expounding, though, if he is at all alert, he can tell when the listeners are merely passive. The question always nagging the lecturer is, "How much is the learner learning?" and he must constantly be devising ways to find out.

The second kind of danger centers upon the lecturer: the whole situation tends to place too much importance upon the single personality of the lecturer. It is much too easy for the learners to regard him as the supreme authority in the field, and this is especially dangerous if he is not, for their rapt attention and lack of verbal challenge may lull the lecturer into the illusion that his words do actually comprise The Word. It is, in short, too easy to get away with a poor job, to get by with information he is not absolutely certain about. It is much too easy, also, for the lecturer to forget the individuality of his learners: they become a "class," and he may even come to speak of the group, for convenience at first, as "it."

To slip into any of these dangers, even without conscious intent, is fatal to Christian teaching. To do so deliberately is to tempt sanity.

* * * *

To combat the disadvantages and to improve the advantages that are inherent in the lecture method, the teacher of Christianity must constantly make two demands of his work.

The lecturer must work consciously with the techniques of presenting his material. He must learn to do everything he can to give a good performance. He will always be on the alert for illustrations. He will learn to introduce and control humor. He will polish his vocabulary until it is not only vivid but also accurate. He will learn how to start with a clang and end with a bang. He will refine his outlines until they are crystal clear, and then he will learn how to handle them to keep interest mounting and produce a climax. He will try to become so much the master of his own techniques that he can always keep one part of his mind focused on the individual learners, ready to pounce upon the flicker of interest in one and recapture the wandering thoughts of another.

He will also constantly work at the material itself. It is his task to combine sound scholarship with popular interest. He must learn how to give a stunning lecture without becoming, himself, the center of the learner's attention. He is to be both authority and interpreter of the material. He will never rest until he has run down the most elusive bit of information. He will be digging at the primary sources behind his interpretation. (Every local church needs a few such scholars, and it is probably the responsibility of the minister to recruit and develop them.) He will try to become so much the master of his subject that he can listen to the class as well as to himself. It is the task of the lecturer in Christianity to be both student and teacher, that is, to stand on both sides of the teaching-and-learning process, for only thus can the monologue of lecturing become the dialogue of address-and-response.

*   *   *   *   *

Lecturing takes many forms, and the teacher of Christianity will make use of a variety of them. The *panel* presentation is a form of lecturing in which there are several lecturers, each chosen for his special interest in or information about a common subject. It is useful in dealing with a many-faceted subject such as sex. The *forum* is another style of lecturing, less formal than the panel, and providing for direct exchange among the lecturers. The engagement of points of view is often informative of the nature of dialogue as well as of the subject itself, and may be very useful in dealing with controversial subjects such as social action. The *debate* is a highly formalized forum, in which the exchange between speakers is carried on according to strictly defined rules of procedure and limits of time. It is especially useful in bringing out information about a technical subject on which there are also sharply defined points of view, such as policy decisions. All these are useful with specially gathered groups of youth and adults for the exploration of special subjects.

There are two other forms of lecturing that are often used by teachers of Christianity with their regular classes: *question-and-answer* teaching, and *assignment-and-recitation* teaching. It is perhaps enough to point out that these are both essentially monological techniques. In the former, the learner is the lecturer, and the teacher asks the questions. It is sometimes called the "tutorial" method of teaching, and was invented by Socrates. It usually consists of leading the student to the conclusion that the tutor already had established. It has often proceeded by exposing the learner's ignorance and piercing his pretensions. It has been used with great effectiveness, especially at Oxford and Cambridge, but usually assumes learners of considerable resilience and independence. If the teacher of Christianity has a special gift for tutorial instruction, he should treasure and develop it carefully, learning what subject matter in the Christian content and what age and situation of learners will respond most effectively to this method. It may very likely be the high school seniors and young adults, and the subject be personal philosophy and ethics. The second form, *assignment-and-recitation,* is used almost universally in church schools, now that prepared curriculum materials from denominational headquarters have become very attractive and plentiful. In this instance, the textbook is the lecturer. The special disadvantage of this form is that the lecturer is impersonal and the teacher's role with the class somewhat ambiguous and unclear. Good teaching may be done in this manner, especially when the Bible is the lecturer, and the class sits before it in order to hear its address. As many adult Bible study groups have discovered, however, while the principle seems impeccable theoretically, it is almost impossible practically to let the Bible be the only teacher in the classroom, and almost inevitably some person less qualified steps in and takes control of the group.

*

The lecture form of the teaching-and-learning dialogue is widely used and is sometimes very effective in the teaching of Christianity. It places emphasis on the objective element in dialogue, the content. The task in lecturing, therefore, is to make the process of presenting the content as personal as possible and to find ways of helping the learners to respond personally, though silently, to the address. It is important that the teacher of Christianity use the lecture method carefully, well, and not exclusively.

10

Storytelling

The telling of stories is a method of enabling the teaching-and-learning dialogue in which one voice reports or recreates the form of dialogue.

The story has been the favorite medium of many great teachers. Plato used it in the Dialogues, brilliantly seductive conversations in which one of the parties is little more than a "straight man" whose job is to raise questions for which the teacher already has answers worked out, to say "yes, indeed," and "please go on," until the reader finds himself thinking along the lines suggested by Plato. The principle of Plato's form of dialogue is that truth is to be found by reasonably examining the meeting of minds. The Hebrew idea of the story centered on acts, their intentions and their results. Thus the stories of the Old Testament relate events more than conversations. The Hebrew writers also turned to the story form when an inexplicable mystery was to be dealt with, and thus, rather than developing a theory about the origin of the universe, they told a story of God's creative acts. The continuous thread of God's activity throughout the stories drew the whole into a "sacred history," in which the truth is to be found in the way men respond to God's acts. Jesus was also a storyteller, and the word "parable" is defined by his telling of them. His stories illustrate the greatest strength of this teaching method: what another teacher would take wearying argument and amplification to state, Jesus enclosed in a single, memorable action. The story was usually interesting in its own right. It could usually be interpreted on several levels of meaning, but Jesus seldom bothered to point to a single one. His stories were symbols: that is, they partook of the reality which they also represented.

The story has been the characteristic method of informal education. It has been universally used by teachers of religion. The teacher of Christianity has, thus, inherited a treasury of teaching stories. History is essentially a series of them. Myth and legend are story forms. Ballads are usually stories, and folktales are often among the best stories there are. All of them have been worked over by countless storytellers until they are as effective in communication and perfect in form as human talent can make them. They have the capacity, when repeated by a good narrator, to transport listeners directly to distant places and faraway times, to bring them into direct relation with unusual ideas and meaningful insights. It has been said that the task of a story is to illuminate life as we know it. It is also the capacity of a story to present life as we do not often know it, but should, were we wise enough. The story is a carrier of the experience of dialogue, itself.

The story is, in short, one of the most familiar and useful tools of the teacher. It is, also, one of the most misused. For both reasons, the teacher of Christianity would do well to become a specialist in the art of storytelling.

*

There is one primary condition for the effective use of the story in teaching-and-learning: a good storyteller. Almost any subject matter will do if only it can be cast into the form of events and conversation, and that is precisely the talent of the storyteller: he sees stories where other people do not see them. Newspaper accounts, street corner events, chance bits of repartee, even his own daydreams —in matters that another man would not even notice, the storyteller finds a yarn that yearns to be spun.

Stories may be told to every age group and sometimes, if they are good enough, to all ages at once. All that is necessary is that the concepts and events, the language and circumstances, be familiar enough to the listeners to provide a basis for listening. A story need not be credible to the listeners, but it does need to be authentic. Even if it be about things completely strange to their daily experiences, it must at least "ring bells" in some corner of their human experience. Stories are not merely for children, though it is recognized that children are story lovers. Though often points may be made in a story of which no amount of abstract reasoning would convince a child, the same may be more true of adults than we often admit.

All that is needed is a storyteller, a story, and an audience. No equipment is needed for storytelling. It is true that stories usually go best in small groups where the contact between the teller and the listeners can be personal and direct, but everyone also knows that stories can be effectively told to vast, and sometimes unseen, audiences. However, stories may be made even more vivid with the use of simple puppets or marionettes, and children are especially fascinated by the concreteness they give to words. A teacher of children would do well to experiment with them.

* *

The storytelling method of teaching-and-learning has some important advantages, but in each of them lurks a danger or, at least, a temptation.

Interest is built into the form by its own nature. "Once upon a time" is a sure signal for attention, and Jesus' memorable "There was a certain man" evokes a readiness from even a bored listener. Everyone knows that what is about to be said will deal with people and things that may happen to them, and that may promise to be much more interesting than the abstract discussion of principles that had just been going on. Knowing this, it is easy for the teacher to yield to the temptation to pull a story out of his bag of tricks whenever interest flags. A story is not a gimmick; it has its own integrity and should not be simply "used."

The capacity for illustration is also built into the story form. It is by nature a condensation of a variety of events and principles into a concrete happening with a central theme. Two principles are therefore to be kept together: a story is an invaluable instrument for making a point, but it should never be made to make a point that is not inherent in it. When the story itself is not clearly understood, its telling may more confuse than clarify the issue to which it is related. "That reminds me" is not always sufficient reason for introducing it.

Imagination is an integral element of the story form, and its use by the storyteller will precipitate its action in the listeners. The story leaps beyond time and place, and the barriers of current convention or traditional concept do not limit its content. Science fiction has been credited with providing a tool for more practical scientific imagination. Listening to stories may literally engage persons in that essential act of dialogue, crossing over to the other side of experience. But though dialogue may be prompted by imagination, it is meaningless unless it occurs in life.

*   *   *

Some of the dangers of the storytelling method of teaching-and-learning have already been suggested.

It is easy to substitute storytelling for actual experience. It is much simpler to tell a story about an interracial experiment than to find a possibility for actual interracial encounter, prepare for it, and carry it through; the story will probably also avoid the attention and criticism that might well be precipitated by direct action. The telling of the story should always be related in some real way to the actual experiencing and doing of the learners.

It is easy, in the same way, to substitute storytelling for information. Especially in the teaching of history, a story is seldom a responsible substitute for historical research, though it may often provide a meaningful supplement to hard facts. It is a great temptation, especially to be watched by the facile storyteller, to substitute tale-spinning for fact-finding.

It is easy, also, to use the story form too much. A story is seldom the whole lesson, as sometimes appears to be the theory of curriculum writers. After all, Christianity is not a story, even though many of its most significant events took place in history and may be effectively retold: Christianity is something that actually happens to people, here and now as well as in distant times and places. The story form must not be so generously used as to convey the impression, to young or old, that Christianity is merely a beautiful story about a baby in a manger, or even merely an agonizing story about the execution of a man outside the city walls. Flesh and blood, joy and suffering are involved, and when *his* story becomes *my* story, my own feelings and acts will be caught up in actual experiences that are far more real than any story.

* * * *

In the teaching of individual lessons, storytelling may serve a variety of functions, and the teacher of Christianity will make use of many of them from time to time. A story is an excellent way of opening a teaching-and-learning session. It can often be used effectively for setting up a discussion, or for searching the imagination of the group and setting it off on a long-term project. It may be used during a session for interpreting an abstract or obscure point. It may be inserted at a point of impasse, to unlock new thinking about the subject. It may serve to dramatize or emphasize the essential lesson of the session. It may be used for summary at the end of the session, lifting out and clarifying the facts unearthed or issues discussed. It may be used at the time of worship, to gather up and direct the thinking of the group toward a single issue. But always, if it is to serve the teaching-and-learning dialogue as it is equipped by its very nature to do, the story will be used in accord with its own inherent point. That is to say, the story will always, when effectively used, be permitted to speak for itself, to tell, as it were, its own story.

*   *   *   *   *

It is incumbent upon the teacher of Christianity, whether he tells stories often or infrequently, to master the form of the story and cultivate the craft of the storyteller.

The effective teaching story is essentially in the "short story" form, of which any good textbook on the subject will provide a helpful discussion. Knowing the classic form analysis of the short story should help the teacher in his selection from the vast literature of stories available. Unfortunately, many in the collections of "Stories for Teachers" will not stand the test of telling, and it is wise for the teacher to learn to know how to recognize a bad story before trying to tell it.

Except for the sonnet, the short story may be the most disciplined form of literary composition. The short story is compressed in size, and is built of three elements: events, conversation, and description. Of these, the last is of least importance, being usually either omitted entirely or carried by the action and conversation themselves. Ordinarily, the story will begin with an explosive event, sometimes called the "precipitating action." It will be relevant to the place, time, and nature of the story, and will introduce the central character first. It may all be contained in a single sentence. If any description is necessary, it will follow this opening event. As a general rule, the story will take place in one time and place and involve no more than three characters, one of whom is protagonist and one of whom is probably antagonist. Simplicity is the key to the effectiveness of the short story. Then comes a sequence of events in a rising arc of interest and ancitipation. If there is conversation, it will ordinarily carry the action forward and be an integral part of it. At the peak of this ascending action comes the climax, which, of course, may be either action or speech or both. The falling action, or denouement, in a short story is quick and fast; its primary purpose is not to further the action so much as to tie up all the loose ends. O. Henry is known for his use of the surprise ending, in which there was no denouement at all. The "moral" is not a part of the short-story form; in general, it is a good guide to assume that if the moral is not clear in the story, the story should not be told. If the teacher feels that it is necessary, for the purposes of the lesson (not the story) to pinpoint the moral, let him do it deftly, without stabbing both it and the story to death.

Telling a story involves far more than a casual recounting of its essentials, and the craft of telling good stories deserves careful cultivation. It is well, at the beginning, to select one's stories from the classic sources and to assume that the story is as well told as it can be, reducing one's own improvements to the minimum. The first step, then, is to become thoroughly familiar with it. This will involve reading it carefully, perhaps aloud, at least a dozen times. The teller should also outline the story, probably in writing, and probably along the lines of the "form" just analyzed. It is necessary, also, to learn to visualize characters and places so that one can see them in his own mind, observing details as if they were present, and being able to describe them vividly. By this time he should be so familiar with the story and its elements that he can feel them going on as he reviews them. This process is sometimes called "internalization." At last he is prepared to practice telling the story aloud, to himself, to his mirror, to the family, to a child he does not know well. Thus, when he comes to telling the story to the class, he will be so thoroughly in command of the *story* that he can tell it to *them*.

*

For the teacher of Christianity, the art of storytelling is one of the most valuable and venerable of methods for enabling the teaching-and-learning dialogue. Its power lies in its embodiment of the elements of encounter. Its effectiveness depends upon the teacher's mastery of its skills, for he must make the living dialogue seem present through his own presentation alone. Its potential lies in the vast store of narrative literature preserved and treasured by the Christian faith and movement. In learning to teach by telling stories, he will have joined voices with the great teachers of history.

11

Visual Aids

The use of visual aids is a method of enabling the teaching-and learning dialogue without relying on voices.

Appealing to the eye rather than to the ear in presenting a message is nothing new, of course. It is as old as stone-age paintings of hunt and worship on the walls of caves. Babylonian hieroglyphic writing was but a highly refined form of communication through pictures, and Navajo sand painting is a sophisticated use of pictures as religious symbols. The last lesson Jesus taught before he was arrested was by neither sermon nor story but by using bread and wine as visual symbols to fix a lesson of deathless meaning. A century ago, in many Protestant churches, the "infant class" was nurtured on vivid pictures of the Bible lesson—Abraham in blue and purple ready to sacrifice a pale green Isaac on a magenta altar with a dark gray lamb caught in the black and red bramble bushes handy by. More recently, other children have been instructed by a picture of an Anglo-Saxon, sandy-haired, blue-eyed Jesus.

The modern phase in the educational use of visual aids began with World War II, during which the U. S. armed forces developed teaching-by-showing to an unprecedented degree. Faced with the need of communicating to hundreds of thousands of men in a minimum period of time, the military called upon Hollywood, and as a result instruction was offered by film in almost everything from field stripping the M-1 rifle to mountain skiing and sex morality. In the building and population boom that followed the war, the public schools went all out for visual aids: courses were offered in the colleges of education, and special pay scales were created in local school districts for teachers who became authorities in materials and equipment. The churches also went on an edifice and equipment binge. Sometimes it seemed that churchmen hoped the kingdom of God might come by projection since it had not yet come by prayer. No church was content until it had projecting equipment, both sound and silent, both still and moving; these necessitated roll-down screens in rooms that can be darkened, ample outlets for electric power and public address systems, libraries of catalogued materials in boxes and cans. Missionary executives even received serious requests from new Christians miles from electric power for projection equipment.

The tragedy of all this enthusiasm is not that it is wrong-headed, for the method of teaching through visual aids rests on sound principles. The first tragedy is that the facilities have never been adequately put to use in functional support of education. There are rich supplies of thirty-five millimeter transparencies on the history of art and architecture of which teachers of Christianity seem quite unaware. Churches have not begun to touch the possibilities for adolescent and adult education in serious "problem" films, both domestic and foreign, and their discussion. A second tragedy has been the bypassing of simpler and less electronic forms of visual aid to the educative process.

The basic principle of visual aids is a refinement of the oriental aphorism that a picture is worth ten thousand words: the attempt is simply to use the eye as well as the ear. Edgar Dale, pioneer of the audio-visual movement in secular education, appropriately puts his basic theory in a picture. It takes the form of a cone, which he labels "experience." There are ten levels. At the broad base are three levels called "doing," and these are the most effective in teaching-and-learning: 1. direct experience; 2. contrived experience; and 3. dramatic participation. The middle section of the cone is labeled "observing" and consists of five levels: 4. demonstration; 5. field trips; 6. exhibits; 7. motion pictures; 8. radio, recording, and still pictures. This middle section of the cone describes the experiences which visual aids seek to utilize. The top and narrow part of the cone is called "symbolizing" and consists of two levels: 9. visual symbols; and 10. verbal symbols. These are said to be the least effective of learning experiences.

The teacher of Christianity should be aware of the potentialities and problems of teaching without words and discover his own capacity to use visual aids in the service of the divine address that came to man first in the flesh and later found its way into sayings.

The use of visual aids obviously necessitates the preparation, maintenance, and use of a certain amount of equipment. It may be a minor affair in the exhibiting of an ancient Palestinian lamp, but even so, the piece must be secured, protected, and returned. In the case of the projecting of a sound film, the projector must be in order and properly set up, the screen arranged, the room darkened and ventilated, the chairs arranged for viewing, the sound system set up and checked. So intricate has all this become that some churches and many schools have specifically equipped one room for audio-visual use and put special personnel in charge of the equipment. When that is done, schedules for the use of the room must be prepared, and, if it becomes much used, they must be arranged long in advance of the actual teaching session. Whether the situation be simple or complex at the beginning, it seems to be the tendency in the use of all forms of visual aids for the equipment to become more rather than less demanding and intricate.

The use of visual aids also requires a certain sort of content: it must be graphic and concrete, or "picturable," if it is to be taught by showing. While the principle may not often present a problem to the teacher of mechanical drawing, the teacher of Christianity must recognize that he is constantly dealing with abstract ideas and spiritual realities that cannot be photographed or diagrammed. The doctrine of the trinity has not always been made more meaningful by charts of circles and triangles, and there is one historic instance in which a late medieval teacher of theology lost a brilliant student and helped to bring to an end his world of thought and values by attempting to visualize the unpicturable: the student was Philip Melanchthon, who had much to do with the German Reformation, and the subject was transubstantiation.

It is obvious that the content must be educationally appropriate

101

to the group with which it is used if the visual aid is to be an effective teaching-and-learning method. So also must be the particular method of representation. Some children who have become bored with movies will be fascinated with slides. An original painting may be more meaningful to some than any number of prints. Many people, both young and old, have never held a very ancient thing in their own hands; to place his own hands in the grooves made by a potter's fingers four thousand years ago may constitute for one learner a direct meeting with that ancient person, and for another be a wasted effort.

Visual aids must be related to the entire process of teaching-and-learning. One of the lessons of World War II was that nobody ever learned to ski by watching filmed instructions. The typical error of church-school teachers is to show a filmstrip to the class merely because it happens to be available, and in spite of the fact that it also happens to have nothing remotely to do with the lesson. The use of a visual aid will never be educationally effective as a gimmick; it is essential that it be treated as seriously as any other element of the curriculum.

*   *

The primary advantage of the visual aid is made clear by the "cone of experience": that which can be experienced visually is more deeply felt than that which is merely verbalized. Christianity is itself an experience rather than a word. It is also true that, because the experience is with the absolute, the Christian content is saturated with concepts and principles that need to be made concrete and immediately present to the learner if it is to have any meaning for him. The life of Jesus becomes far more personal and meaningful when the learner has some sense of the spaces, the climate, and the culture of Palestine. It is important that the modern Protestant have some understanding of "the medieval mind," an abstract generalization that can be given flesh and blood by an encounter with paintings, buildings, and the smell and dangers of medieval life. Love may remain an abstract principle unless it is brought to sight and life by illustrations from both far and near. The teacher of Christianity may use visual aids to illustrate, to clarify, to concretize. They are also interest getters. There is nothing quite like a picture or an artifact to start the endless chain of questions—"What is it?" "Where did it come from?" "What was it for?" "Who is that?" "Why is he dressed that way?"—that becomes the outline for today's lesson.

*　　*　　*

There are also dangers in the use of this powerful method of teaching-and-learning. One of them concerns the equipment, which may for one teacher be a constant source of problems and headaches, and for another become so fascinating that all his attention is absorbed by it: in both cases, the essential educational process is interfered with by the insertion of an impersonal thing into the midst of the personal teacher-and-learner relationship.

Other dangers lurk in the nature of the method. Knowing that a visual aid is a powerful teaching device, some teachers are tempted to assume that the teaching function of an object or picture is self-evident. Even visual aids must be "taught," and mere displaying is seldom teaching. Knowing that the visual aid is strong because it lies nearer the level of direct experiencing than words, other teachers are tempted to assume that seeing a movie about the dilemma of underpaid workers in slum housing is just as effective an experience as actually visiting the slum area just a block behind the church building. Visual aids should never be used to substitute for direct experiences except when the experiences themselves are unavailable. And, knowing that visual aids require time for mechanical preparation as well as for presentation, some teachers yield to the temptation to substitute the use of visual aids for preparation of the content matter itself. There is nothing quite so ineffectual and, because it has happened so often as to become a joke, quite so pathetic as the teacher who presents a movie he knows nothing about to a class that has no way to know anything about it. The usual result is that the film makes an entirely different point from that which the teacher had supposed it might; when the lights come on, there he stands, with his announced purpose in shreds.

A problem attaching especially to the use of movies has to do with mass communication and the tabloid mind. The Christian dialogue is always one-to-one, it can never be depersonalized and achieved on a mass scale. The Christian faith is seldom merely entertaining. The Christian experience cannot be reduced to a series of animated cartoons. There must always be specific educational reason for the use of a visual aid, and the canned form must not be so much used as to turn the teaching-and-learning of Christianity into a sideshow for spectators only.

*   *   *   *

Visual aids take many forms, and the teacher of Christianity will do well to cultivate a knowledge of the resources available to him.

Objects, specimens, and models comprise a class of teaching aids that is often overlooked. Museums are a source of artifacts from other cultures, both contemporary and ancient; with proper assurances curators will often loan materials for use in the classroom, and trips to the museum itself can always be arranged. A church school should encourage the making of good models, and then preserve and reuse them: the temples and forts, towns and houses, cooking utensils, ovens, and clothing from all points of church history. A full-scale Palestinian house with working equipment might be as useful a project as the house-making corner with which almost every kindergarten is equipped. In certain climates a Palestinian garden can be grown.

Graphic materials comprise another category of aids: maps, graphs, time lines, posters, blackboards, bulletin boards. These may be familiar to most teachers of Christianity. Yet chalk boards and bulletin boards frequently hang unused in church school classrooms; teachers should learn how to use them effectively. Every church school should have a major map of Palestine, the "fertile crescent," the Mediterranean basin, the world. These might cover entire walls, be constructed in relief and painted by local experts, and be used constantly by all age groups. Time lines are an absolute necessity in the teaching of any historical subject, and many have been made clumsily and lost eventually; a first-class, well-illustrated, permanent time line might not only be an excellent visual aid, but also an example toward which others might work in making their own.

Because so much of the objective content of Christianity has to do with distant and strange places, every church school should be constantly building a file of pictures. It should be selective, catalogued, and available. The rich store of paintings by master artists of the Christian story is often almost completely ignored. Excellent prints of many of them are available and inexpensive, and the classroom should be kept alive with good paintings appropriate to the subject under study. Changing good paintings often may be a more important guide to the nature of Jesus than hanging a single one forever with the implied authority of one artist's vision and technique.

*

Visual presentation is a fascinating, effective, and abundant source of aid to the teaching-and-learning process. There is no practical reason that the teacher's presentations of content should not glow with visual illustrations. The teacher of Christianity should still be engaged in the art of illuminating manuscripts. Dialogue is not, however, built on gadgets alone, and the temptation to become the servant of equipment and gimmicks must be resisted. The teacher of Christianity is dedicated to the enabling of a dialogue of divine-human acts, and in a world overflowing with the din of impersonal words, he will do well to explore methods of teaching without words what is beyond words.

12

Discussion

The discussion method of teaching-and-learning is an attempt to enable dialogue by using a verbal form of dialogue, conversation.

Conversations take place at a variety of levels of importance. Many of the casual exchanges of daily life—a few pleasant words about the weather, the firm assertions in passing that one is feeling "fine"—are not only relatively meaningless, but often are outright deceptions as well, for the weather is actually quite unpleasant and both conversants are really feeling terrible and both know that neither cares. Other conversations are memorable for their meaningfulness and rarity—wartime buddies meet after twenty years of separation and immediately their relationship is as direct and intimate as if they had never been apart; two well-known physicists who have never met before but have admired each other's work in books and articles spend a day in earnest talk; a husband and wife plan the family vacation. These occasions come much closer to the meaning of the word conversation, carrying with them some of the depth suggested in the idea of "the converging of opposites in discourse."

Discussion is merely prearranged, directed, or formalized conversation, and it, too, may take place at different levels of meaning. A discussion may be no more than a form of gossip, or an exchange of ignorance. It may consist merely of going 'round and 'round in logical and emotional circles. It may be chiefly an argument among points of view, in which strategy is paramount and the entire purpose is to win advantage or convince an opponent. Or discussion may take the form of a genuine conference among independent minds and wills in which the accepted purpose of all parties is to find the solution to a common problem. On this level, discussion is a demanding and exciting method of group thinking. It is of this prospect that a college co-ed once said: "Oh, we're going to have a discussion? Well, I'll have to leave: thinking gives me a headache."

Recently there has been much discussion of discussion. Big business and big government have discovered the potentiality of group thought, and with the bureaucratic tendency to assume that two minds are always better than one, have gone all out for it as a method of decision making. The ideal is said to be that no one knows, when it is all over, who suggested the germinal idea that solved the problem. The trick is "to put ideas in the hat," "kick the ball around," "get out the bugs," and "lay all the cards on the table," in order to "break the logjam" and "get the juices flowing again," until something finally "rings the bell."

In educational theory, discussion puts the emphasis on participation rather than on presentation. The lecture, storytelling, and visual aids are all presentations by the teacher to the learners. Discussion, group activities, and creative dramatics are all teaching-and-learning methods in which the teacher and the learners participate together in the educative process. Frequently their distinctive roles, so clearly defined always in the presentational forms of teaching, have less to do with educational rank and more to do with individual contributions. Question-and-answer and recitation-and-report teaching are intermediary forms between presentation and participation.

The teacher of Christianity senses that discussion is in the same form as the dialogue he seeks to open for his learners. Both involve a meeting of persons, a speaking and a listening and a responding, a giving and a receiving and a sharing. It is therefore a method of teaching-and-learning he will study and practice. However, since it is a form of dialogue and not the thing itself, he may be called upon to exercise special disciplines lest the form become confused with the reality.

*

A meaningful discussion presupposes a vital and concrete situation or problem. Failing to meet this essential condition is the usual reason for that frustrating experience so often passed off with the gallant comment, "Well, we didn't reach any conclusions today, but we had a great discussion." The two parts of that assertion are, probably, mutually exclusive, but whether or not there has been any conclusion achieved, there can never be a good discussion without something at the heart of it—or of the group—worth chewing on. In other words, not every subject is discussible. The limitations of most subjects are built in; it is quite normal that for most people the weather is a subject that can be talked about only briefly and inconclusively. For an educational discussion, the subject must have its own potential.

Meaningful discussion also demands a skillful leader. The primary responsibility of the leader in discussion is not to withdraw, but rather to prod, inform, and lead until some sort of learning breakthrough is assured, and he can withdraw without endangering that achievement, whatever the final conclusions may be. The teacher who uses the discussion method must therefore possess a thorough knowledge of the problem under discussion; indeed, it may be necessary for him to know the subject so well that he is free to leave the final result to the group. This knowledge is usually boned up by specific preparation. The teacher must also possess certain skills in the guidance of group thought. In general this is composed of two parts. The first, and more important, is a genuine respect for personality. This implies that he will not only try to make it possible for everyone to make his unique contribution, but that he will respect the individuality of the active listener, or the one who does not want to offer a verbal contribution. It implies, also, that he will encourage the criticism of half-formed thoughts and false information. The other factor is fertility of suggestion. The teacher always carries the responsibility for blocking off fruitless avenues, identifying confusing tangents, pointing out fallacies. He can frequently, if he knows how, do this by asking questions. He is also responsible for suggesting new ways to attack ·the problem and additional aspects of the question, for summing up and reviewing and clarifying. And all this he must be able to do without dominating the group or seeking to guide it toward preconceived conclusions.

Resources are also required for meaningful discussion. If there is any single shoal on which most discussions founder, it is probably the lack of information; every discussion repeatedly reaches the point beyond which it cannot proceed further, even with shallow draft, without some facts. Guessing is fatal. It would be better to disband the group than to give support to the notion that satisfactory solutions to important questions can be reached in this life without data. It might not be inappropriate, therefore, to define discussion as "an exchange of information." Since it is impossible to know what directions the interplay of group thought may take, the room in which discussion takes place regularly might well be the library. If this cannot be arranged, the group must provide, for each discussion session, as many resources as possible. Reference works are especially valuable—the Bible in various translations, dictionaries, encyclopedias, and maps.

Time is an essential element for discussion. Few discussions of any subject of merit can be concluded in a half hour. Usually only frustration results from short discussions. Especially with adolescents and adults, two or three hours is a more appropriate length than the usual class session provides.

Some groups may lack the group loyalty, analytical skills, and capacity to verbalize and share. If so, they are candidates for learning these requisites rather than for the discussion method itself.

*　　*

There are significant advantages in the discussion method of teaching-and-learning. The first is that no special equipment is needed. It is helpful to have a quiet room with a table around which to gather and on which to spread out the books and papers. The alert teacher will attempt to provide such a place. But meaningful discussion may sometimes be held as well under the trees or on a street corner as in a seminar room. Indeed, sometimes the best setting for discussion is one in the midst of the problem itself. And the second advantage has to do with the essential similarity between the goal in teaching Christianity and the discussion method. In participating in earnest and informed discussion, the learner is actually learning by doing. In this case he is learning to respect others and their opinions, to cross over to the other's side of the question, to trust the interplay of minds and ideas. This is the real ground of the experience of meeting, and it is holy ground.

*   *   *

There are also disadvantages, and discussion is not to be hastily seized upon as the single and exclusive strategy for the teacher of Christianity. Discussion takes time, and time is precisely what most learners have the least capacity to give. Scheduling new and generous units of time into the busy lives of businessmen, housewives, and school children is often a discouraging undertaking, but it must be done if discussion is to be worthwhile. If capsule education in small doses is all that the teacher of Christianity is permitted, he may do well to turn to a presentational method.

The discussion method of teaching-and-learning is often the occasion for one of the greatest single hazards of the teacher—an argument with a learner. When the lines are suddenly drawn, and the teacher and the learner face each other belligerently across the chasm of disagreement, the teacher must be ready. He must continue to use his own insight and knowledge forthrightly; he cannot submit to the temptation to evade the issue or spread false ointment. He must be so sensitive to this learner, who is probably younger and less experienced, that he can enable him to see the argument through to its natural end. He must not take up a position or conduct a logical maneuver instead of pressing the real and more difficult battle for the truth. He must at the same time be ready to see the validity of his opponent's position if forced, or, even more difficult, to accept a truthful insight or relevant datum in his opponent's argument without granting validity to the whole position. He must be willing to win or lose the argument, knowing that neither will be easy. Entering completely and without reservation into the conflict, he must be aware of the learning potential in the situation for the entire group.

The discussion method contains certain built-in temptations for the teacher. The failure to find a solution, or even to make identifiable progress toward the goal, is one of the constant dangers of the discussion method. Learners become easily discouraged and often request a return to a more presentational method. On the other side of this danger is the temptation for the teacher to force the discussion through to some sort of climax, or even to suggest that a conclusion has been reached when it has not. There is also the temptation for the teacher to substitute the discussion method of teaching for preparation: "There is no telling where this discussion may go today, so what's the use of preparing? I'll just wait and see—and hope I'll have an idea." Leading a discussion requires more preparation than giving a lecture, precisely because "there is no telling. . . ." There is the temptation for the teacher to think, and thus to teach the learners, that adjustment of point of view is the goal of the process. Compromise is not the Christian standard of truthfulness. Use of the discussion method without real discipline has actually led to this secularized and sub-Christian conclusion. Finally, there is the temptation to the skilled discussion leader to do so brilliant a job that learners are led to suppose that the electric give-and-take they have achieved in their sessions together is the full extent of the Christian dialogue. Discussion is a horizontal form of the divine-human dialogue and must never be substituted for the reality itself.

* * * *

Ordinarily, a discussion session will assume a series of distinct shapes, and the teacher of Christianity will do well to be aware of this succession as the discussion progresses. An analysis of form should also help to identify the role of some of the more catchy and foreshortened applications of the discussion technique, such as "buzz groups" (in which a large assembly of people, at a rally for example, is arbitrarily broken up into small sections to talk for an arbitrary period of time about a question and report subsequently to the whole session), or "brainstorming" (in which every participant is encouraged to verbalize the wildest possible approaches to the problem at hand and the inflexible ground rule is that no idea is too bizarre to be accepted). It might help in understanding the difference between a "discussion group" (in which the problem is "over against" the whole group, no matter how personally involved in it members may be) and the "therapy group" (in which the problems are all individually internal). It might even be useful in developing a creative and educative approach to the committee work of the local church.

At the first stage, the members of the group place the problem under consideration in their midst. Whether it be a conceptual theological idea or a concrete problem of ethical behavior, the learners literally gather around it and look at it. This stage might be called *exploration*.

At some point, perhaps now and perhaps later, the problem should be *internalized*. Here the learners try to get inside the problem, to understand, in so far as possible, how it "feels" within. If it is an objective sort of problem, imaginative techniques may be required. If it is a personal sort of problem, it may literally be possible to cross over to the inside of it and feel it from another point of experience.

Then the group takes the problem apart for *analysis*. At this stage the learners line up, as it were, over against the problem and attempt to achieve a common understanding of its elements.

Now, with the problem split up into manageable bits, each of the learners does his own work on some part of it. He may even take it home with him, so to speak. This stage may be called *research*. Relevant information is the goal.

The next stage might be labeled *discovery*. Each learner now has some information or idea to contribute. The group regathers, the contributions are placed in the midst of the group, and the whole problem is seen in a new light.

The most demanding and imaginative stage of the discussion now occurs, *synthesis*. Here the group gathers around and literally puts the problem back together again. From this reassembly of the parts, illuminated with individual contributions, a new pattern should emerge. This is the turning point of the process. It may take the most time. It may be discouraging and frustrating. The group is challenged to remain together until the synthesis has been achieved. If synthesis is impossible, it is necessary to go back to one of the earlier steps and retrace and supplement or correct the process.

The climax is now at hand: *decision*. In the teaching-and-learning situation, it is always useful for the leader to guide the group in a review of the steps and an evaluation of the process of discussion, itself. For the teacher of Christianity, the process is not complete until the decision has been carried into some overt action of dialogue, and the vertical potentialities of the horizontal engagement have been realized.

*

Discussion is a method of teaching-and-learning full of demands and dangers. The teacher of Christianity need not, however, be discouraged about using it. It is one of the characteristics of contemporary culture and the educational approach of the public schools that people—children as well as adolescents and adults—are remarkably well equipped for meaningful participation in discussion learning.

The pity is that the society that has prepared them for it has offered them so little opportunity to practice it. This may constitute the second most powerful reason there is for the teacher of Christianity to practice the art of leading discussions. The other reason is that it is a human model of the divine-human dialogue.

13

Group Activities

Teaching-and-learning through group activities is an effort to enable dialogue through active participation in purposeful sharing.

"Learning by doing" is a concept introduced to modern schools by the progressive education movement. Everywhere in the world, and preeminently in the United States, the idea is linked with the

117

name of John Dewey. For Dewey, the solving of problems by active experimentation in a group was the practical basis for all learning. Even further, experimental activity was, in Dewey's pragmatic philosophy, the actual basis for human experience, intelligence, language, and culture. In everything, he insisted, acts are primary and all else that characterizes man is built out of learning that certain acts produce certain satisfactory or unsatisfactory results. Life is constantly changing. Mind is not an organ but an instrument for adjusting to those changes. Ideas are not innate or absolute, as Plato taught, but the result of action and are to be tested, not by logic, but by the changes produced. Both science and education begin with a problem and follow the same process of observation, analysis, hypothesis, experiment, solution. Education is, therefore, not a preparation for life, but a meaningful experience of life itself. It is essentially a process of trial and error exercised on real problems under the guidance of a teacher in a constantly changing world. Its purpose is not the acquisition of knowledge, but rather the increase of efficiency in solving problems. Schoolrooms should be places in which children can live and will be equipped with benches and tools and materials for working, rather than with desks for listening, slates for copying, and textbooks for memorizing. Children will study, not "Readin', Ritin', and 'Rithmetic," but How Language Began, What Numbers Do, Life in a Medieval Village, and, generally, How a Democratic Society Works.

John Dewey's educational ideas, hammered out practically in the University of Chicago Experimental School in the early years of the century, and refined philosophically in his classrooms at Columbia University Teachers' College in the next thirty years, precipitated a major educational revolution throughout the world. Historians remembered that Pestalozzi had created schools in Switzerland in which the atmosphere of the home was nurtured as a context for beginning to learn all kinds of lessons by starting with loving and being loved. Froebel had begun a movement in Germany for children's schools in which informality and learning by doing were keynotes. In Italy, Montessori was having children begin by relating to "real things." It was chiefly because of the work of Dewey and his disciples, however, that teaching was focused on the learner rather than on the content, learning on action rather than on absorption, education on the process rather than on the result. It is still appropriate to say, as it was often claimed during the 1920's, that John Dewey changed the schools of America from a place where children were bored to death to a place where life begins.

All this, of course, had a tremendous effect on Christian education, especially in the United States. There was ample evidence that children were, in fact, being bored by the listening, copying, and memorizing they were required to do in church schools. All this objective learning seemed to many churchmen to have too little to do with the Christian life, especially in churches swept by the challenge to do something practical about the injustices of society under the leadership of the social gospel and to say something relevant to a scientific culture under the guidance of liberal theology. Church school classrooms, almost suddenly, seemed to become workshops where tiny Palestinian villages were built and salt paste maps of the Holy Land were constructed. Some became headquarters for social welfare activities in depressed neighborhoods.

Unquestionably, Christianity is as much a style of life as a set of propositions. Before they were called "Christians," the disciples of Jesus called themselves "Followers of the Way." One of the most effective ways Jesus used to fix his message in the lives of his followers was to send them out to preach and practice the Good News by doing the Good News. Plato had an Academy to which pupils came to hear him lecture; what we know of his teaching comes chiefly through the accidentally surviving notes taken by his pupils. What we know of Jesus comes largely through seventy generations of people who have tried to do as he did. Christians have always learned Christianity by practicing Christianity. The teacher of Christianity will find ways to bring the actual experiencing of dialogue into the classroom.

*

Learning-by-doing is one of the most demanding and fragile forms of the teaching-and-learning relationship.

First, and most important, there must be a skillful leader. He must constantly be all things to all parts and components of the rapidly moving, dynamic process. To the learners, he must necessarily be a companion in the activity. Learning the art of interhuman engagement requires the complete participation of everyone in the group; it is not necessary, or to be expected, of course, that everyone will participate at the same level, or make the same sort of contribution, but there is no place in the process for an objective nonparticipant. One hold-out can hold up the entire group's experience. Special skill is required for an adult to participate with seven-year-olds in the development of a Thanksgiving liturgy without threatening to invade their originality and dominate their result. He must be able to be an honest companion with them in their whole quest. At the same time, he must be able to act as the guide when the group needs prodding or assistance. At the beginning, it was probably the teacher who inspired the whole project, and laid before the class—not yet a working group!—the possibilities of corporate endeavor in such a realistic way that the class elected to undertake it. At the end, he may be called upon to bring the whole thing through to a satisfactory outcome, to patch up the clumsy map-making of eight-year-olds without insulting them, to sum up the lessons learned without withdrawing from the group and suddenly becoming pedantic. He must, in short, be the sort of leader who is able to teach by letting the process do the teaching, the kind of instructor who is willing not to be called "Teacher," or even "Mister," the rare type of teacher who is willing to be loved by the class as one of them.

There must also be a problem of sufficient scope and depth to sustain learning-by-doing. It must be real, both in itself and to the group. Classes will not be patient long with artificial or theoretical projects. The problem to be solved must have space in it for moving about, size enough for numerous solutions. It must be the sort to which active experiment is appropriate, a practical problem that can actually be worked at but which will not surely defeat the class. All the care in defining it must be used that a scientist uses in defining and limiting his laboratory experiments.

A certain amount of equipment will be required. What and how extensive it must be will depend upon the project, of course. Some projects can be carried on entirely within the classroom, but it will be the teacher's responsibility to gather the paste, cardboard, paints, easels, and smocks. It may be his task, also, to provide for protecting the room so that the entire project will not be interrupted in its midst by a distressed trustee. Some projects will necessarily take place in a larger laboratory—the changing interracial neighborhood, for example; here it will become the teacher's responsibility to anticipate innumerable details before and during the project.

Learning-by-doing takes time. In this respect, it is probably the most demanding of any form of education. Indeed, if the project does seize upon the imagination of the learners and has been adequately designed, the largest difficulty may be to control the time the group wishes to lavish upon it in the interests of the learners' other responsibilities, so that the entire project will not be interrupted in its midst by distressed parents. Enough time must be provided at each session so that a unit or element of the work may be started, worked through, and brought to a conclusion. In addition to a sheer bulk of time, the teacher needs a sense of timing. In view of the difficulty of finding large spaces of time, the teacher may need also to be something of an efficiency expert to see that time is not wasted. The whole point of all this management is simply to provide the learners with a sense of spaciousness for the project so that it may be followed through on their own learning schedule.

For the project method to succeed, there must be a group of learners who can work together or can learn how to do so. Beyond the successful completion of the project itself, there is the more important lesson of working personal relationships to be learned. But this is a delicate process, and it must be recognized that while a working group can perform wonders in transforming noncooperative attitudes, there is a limit to what it can absorb. The mystery of dialogue is the goal of the process, and while the miracle cannot be assured, the possibility should be protected. Ordinarily, also, the group must be limited in size. At the Experimental School, Dewey kept the teacher-learner ratio at 1-10, and some church schools have insisted on one teacher to six or seven learners.

* *

That the learning-by-doing method enables effective learning has been spectacularly demonstrated. The Chicago "Quiz Kids" of radio fame were a direct product of progressive, child-centered, experimental education. Intelligent children in special programs have leaped far ahead of their peers in conventional schools. The approach has been applied to mentally and physically handicapped children with great success in leading them toward independent and adjusted living. No one who has seen a well-led experimental class at work in the church school on the culture and life of an ancient Hebrew town, for example, can fail to be impressed. Parents have been utterly amazed at the change in attitudes wrought in their adolescents by a summer work project among Mexican migrant workers. The undebatable effectiveness of learning-by-doing is due to the fact that data and skills are acquired by total involvement: lessons are not learned by the mind alone but literally by the whole body, all the senses, the entire experience. Facts become part of life.

The teacher of Christianity will be especially sensitive to the potentialities implicit in an approach which proposes that the actual experiencing of dialogue is the best learning of dialogue. The response to the address of God may be described, illustrated, and discussed brilliantly, but nothing of importance happens until the response is actually made. Willingness to think about it and even to try may be encouraged by the experiences of others, but perhaps the most effective way to learn to take the risk of responding to God is to practice actual response to other human beings in the undertaking of common tasks and projects. One learns to love by being among those who love. Dialogue is learned by practicing the arts of addressing and responding in the events of life.

*   *   *

In practice, however, it has been discovered that there are real dangers in the learning-by-doing method for the teacher of Christianity.

It is easy for a teacher so to succumb to the activity method that he will place excessive emphasis on sheer activity, letting it become an end in itself. Moving about does not necessarily develop the mind or the spirit. "We kept busy today" is not necessarily an indication that anything more has been accomplished than to fill the time. It is easy to become so enamored of the method that the teacher never pauses to ask about the educational value of the activities. The word "busy-work" was invented by critics to say that much that happened in the activity classroom was time-filling rather than mind-filling. Public schools that have succumbed to these dangers have learned to fear the cry, "but my Johnny can't read." And church schools have sometimes found to their dismay that they have on their hands college-age students who know nothing of any objective importance about the content of the Bible and the essence of the Christian beliefs.

There is the subtle danger that the activity teacher will allow the busy-ness of the learners to obscure the demands the method places upon him for teaching. The kind of preparation required of him is very different from preparing for a lecture. For this kind of teaching, he needs a lifetime of preparation, a constant awareness of the subject, a rich fund of books, and people at his fingertips and call. He must be so well in command of them that he can supply them on the instant needed. It is easy to forget that it is his responsibility to assure educational progress if it does not come naturally.

Though these dangers to the learning process are real, there are two others inherent in the activity program itself that may be fatal to the goal of dialogue. One arises from the concentration of the method on the group: it is easy to become so engrossed in the overall project and in the functioning of the group that the individual learner is forgotten. The address is ultimately individual, and the response is singular. Dialogue is never we-thou, or we-it. The other fatal danger arises from the concentration of the method on the activity: it is easy to forget that human activity multiplies sin and resistance as often as righteousness and response. Christianity is not a bootstrap religion in which human undertakings are by themselves redemptive. The activity may provide the ground out of which response can arise, but the response is not caused so much by human doings as by God's presence in them.

*   *   *   *

Learning-by-doing takes a variety of forms, and the teacher of Christianity will use many of them in the course of time as he practices the art of dialogue with his learners.

At the lowest level of physical activity is the seminar. Because the activity is chiefly verbal and intellectual, the seminar resembles a discussion group. It is distinguished, however, by the research that takes place, which is usually conducted by task groups and sometimes involves going out into the field to find the information needed. The seminar method works best with adolescents and adults.

Trips and expeditions are a form of learning-by-doing. Meeting with other groups, visiting historic sites, exploring cultural situations different from one's own, worshiping with other religious traditions, are all ways of supplementing listening by doing.

Artistic and constructive projects involve learning-by-doing. Murals, mosaics, maps, and models, when designed and carried through by the group itself, are all appropriate. Especially with primary and junior children, these projects are often occasions for learning both content and relationships.

More extensive group projects have often been high points of participational learning for adolescents and young adults. Building roads in Mexican villages, constructing summer camp facilities for underprivileged children, restoring flood-damaged homes, tutoring illiterate adults, registering Negroes for voting: in sharing the weariness and danger, the concern and sacrifice of demanding projects like these, the life and content of the Christian faith have often been acted and learned.

*

Learning-with-doing is both a modern method of education and a classic strategy for the Christian faith. In both, it has had revolutionary results. In education, it has meant the grounding of intellectual knowledge in whole experience. For Christianity, it has provided a way of linking facts and doctrines to attitudes and values. For the teacher of Christianity, it promises a strategy for conducting the teaching-and-learning session that consists of practicing living dialogue. He will use it carefully and humbly, for both its risks and rewards are great.

14

Dramatics

Creative dramatics is a way of enabling dialogue through creating an artistic form of dialogue.

Aristotle defined all art as imitation and drama as the imitation of an action. In educational dramatics, the emphasis is on the imitation—the imaginative and active recreation of events and

127

conversations by the whole group. In the teaching of Christianity, the emphasis is on the original action of address-and-response between God and man, which the group seeks to relive in the form of the concrete man-to-man dialogue of events and conversations. The imitation of an action is not the action itself, of course, and the group is thus enabled simultaneously to be involved in the recreative action and to stand outside it, observing and evaluating. In this double fact lies the basis for two phenomena: the function of drama as an art form, and the function of creative dramatics as an educational form.

Religion and drama came out of the shadows of prehistory hand in hand. At the moment the first man on some distant dawn crept out of his cave after a night of storm and terror and lifted his arms to the sun in gratitude for new life, both religion and drama were born. Little by little these acts of thanksgiving, and others of petition, were stylized into ritual. Later, stories about the mystical engagement between light and dark, the spirit of life departing during the winter to return in glory in the spring, the struggle of life against death, were developed and enacted with human performers. Even in the Golden Age of Greece with its highly developed society, massive amphitheaters, and technically advanced productions, drama was essentially one with religion, and theater days were religious festivals. In the early Christian period, the mass became a reenactment of the Lord's Supper, and later, the action was no longer considered an imitation but an actual event in which bread and wine were mystically transformed into flesh and blood. In the Middle Ages, drama was one of the teaching agencies of the church, and later of the guilds and towns. Only in the more recent periods of the Puritan and the Rationalist were drama and religion separated as functions of distinct and competing institutions: theater and church.

Among the Jews and the early Christians, the distinction between act and imitation was never made, and art forms as such, including theater, never arose. Life was neither dull nor artless, however, because acts themselves possessed an authenticity standing for the total involvement of the person who acted. Religion itself took on special beauty and excitement because it was understood to be the living acts of God among men and the living acts of men in response. Hebraic religion was neither a drama nor theatrical, but it was dramatic to the core. The life, passion, and resurrection of Jesus comprised an original, dramatic event: there was no play-acting, no prepared script, no imitation. In them God and man and a Man interacted for the salvation of man and the fulfillment of God's purpose. The account of all these acts in both Old and New Testaments is drama, in an essential sense. To teach the Bible dramatically, therefore, is to teach its own nature. To remember and relive these events is to participate in that drama in an artistic sense. To enable new acts of dialogue to spring into life in one's own existence is to teach-and-learn Christianity.

Most teachers of Christianity will find occasions on which creative dramatics will seem to be the most effective form of enabling dialogue. Some teachers of special gifts will find it their usual way of conducting a teaching-and-learning session. In either case, teachers will discover it to be one of the most rigorous, demanding, and exciting of group processes.

*

If creative dramatics is to be an effective method of teaching-and-learning, the purpose in undertaking it must be to develop persons and deepen their understanding, not to produce a show. Drama is a very different thing in the commercial theater, or even in a classroom on theater production from what it is in a classroom where the immediate subject is the flight from Egypt. Each may deepen a sense of participation in life, but in the latter drama is neither an end-in-itself nor a thing-in-itself, but rather a means to the learning of something else.

The content must, of course, be a story or situation sufficiently credible and profound to sustain dramatic development. The best plays are usually comprised of events that happen among people and illustrate principles, rather than of conversations and ideas alone, no matter how witty and brilliant the playwright may be in contriving talk. The same is true of creative dramatics in the classroom, especially when the class is younger children.

The group of learners must be capable of cooperative group planning and working, and probably even of sustaining interest over an extended period of time. This is to suggest that if the dramatic project is to be of any length or intricacy, the group probably needs to be prepared by experiences with other group projects before plunging into creative dramatics.

Creative dramatics, as all sorts of learning processes, requires resources. An unbelievable amount of information will be required, even before the project can get well under way, about conditions, climate, and geography; about customs, dress, and speech; about story, setting, and characters; to say nothing of how best to portray the ideas, tell the events, arrange the groupings, manage the sequences, build the climaxes. People with some experience in technical production, theater direction, and costume making will be useful. Reference books should be at hand. One can never be really prepared for what may be needed in such a project, but he should never begin unprepared.

*   *

The advantages of teaching-and-learning through creative dramatics are many, but the most important have to do with the possibilities for whole, personal development.

Dramatic play is so natural to human beings, especially in childhood, that it is sometimes said to be "instinctive." At every age of life there is some level at which the individual achieves respite from action and thus maintains a balance of things-and-spirit by playing a role rather than being "himself." Children cope with loneliness, adolescents find themselves, adults experiment with solutions to problems, through imaginative play. For most people, living in a world where public mistakes are strictly rationed in number and importance, dramatic play is a form of thinking, a way of exploring and solving problems. Thus the educational process simply formalizes what most people need and want to do, anyway. The chief trick is to find the kind of dramatic play most suitable to the age group with which one is dealing.

Participation in creative dramatics involves the individual in balancing subjective and objective, "inside" and "outside" experiences. This is an essential area of personal development, and the fact that it is insufficiently explored is often the cause of deep-seated personal problems. In acting, the individual is involved in self-identification in regard to another personality. Playing any role helps one to understand himself, in the most helpful way possible, that is, by clarifying who he is in relation to someone else. Because the other person in this instance is the character he is playing, the actor-learner is more free than he can ever be with a real, here-and-now person to feel that other experience from the inside, to cross over to that other side of experience and participate wholly, if briefly and somewhat artificially, in it. The individual is also involved in self-identification in regard to the whole group of persons in the play and the objective story and events of the plot. He cannot play his role alone, and his character is limited by certain agreed traits and his actions by a certain story. He is thus enabled to see himself and what he is doing from the outside, to stand off and look at his own creation from the point of view of the group and its aims.

Creative dramatics also takes advantage of several special opportunities. The self is wholly involved, thought as well as emotion, large physical activities as well as detailed analysis. Every talent, from miming to sewing, is put to use. Imagination is called into play and stretched at every step. Drama is perhaps the most disciplined of all group processes, and imposes its own demands upon the entire group. Rehearsals offer the chance to repeat an action, "rerun it," for evaluation and analysis and correction. In all these ways, the entire capacity and experience of every individual is exercised, and this total involvement means educational effectiveness.

*   *   *

There are also disadvantages and dangers in the use of creative dramatics as a teaching-and-learning strategy. It is very easy for the project to get out of hand.

Every form of drama requires time and devotion, and educational dramatics can be no exception. Sometimes a simple dramatic event —perhaps a posed picture of Jesus' harassment of the money changers in the temple at Jerusalem—may be accomplished and explored in a half-hour, but even so, it must be admitted that the event could be described by a good lecturer in sixty seconds, or somebody else's picture of it shown in fifteen. In addition, a great deal of freedom is needed for the group to work productively, and this may involve more liberty with the content material or in group behavior than the teacher is willing to grant or the situation permits.

There is an indefinable point at which creative dramatics becomes theater, and it is often not only difficult to recognize the point but almost impossible to stop the development. Creative dramatics is not drama for drama's sake, but drama for the sake of learning. Perhaps the greatest catastrophe when educational dramatics becomes drama for drama's sake is the seriously wrong ideas about professional theater that the members of the group are prone to cherish—for example, that acting is merely the assuming of some outward characteristics, that one is really a good actor himself because he seemed to do well as King Saul, that theater is always the same sort of pure, impassioned search for truth and relationship that the class has experienced, that the biblical events are something like costumes that can be put on and taken off at one's own will and convenience. These are much more serious failings than the very corny plays, judged by any sort of objective standards, that are sometimes produced.

There is also the danger of succeeding too well in making the process exciting and rewarding. On the one hand, the experience of representing dialogue may be taken for the experience of dialogue itself. The purpose of the whole project is, indeed, to enable learners to hear the voice of God, but Jim Smith's uncertain adolescent quaver from the wings is not the divine address, even though the script explicitly says *Voice of God* beside Jim's line, and the sense of group accomplishment, interpersonal candor, and wholehearted dedication to a common cause, even at its best is only a human creation, inspiring and valid though it may be. Especially if the wondrous breakthrough of human limitations should occur and be identified, there is the other danger that it will tend to cut out nonparticipants rather than to take them in and to share its excitement. In this event, the result challenges the validity of the group process itself.

* * * *

Creative dramatics is primarily distinguished by its concentration on the nontheatrical learning experience, and within this definition it can take a variety of forms from simple to complex. The simplest, perhaps, is *dramatic play,* in which five-year-olds, for example, play out the roles of Mother and Father in the housekeeping corner of the kindergarten room. With a little suggestion, these undirected scenes may be turned to the exploration and development of relationships. Characters, words, costumes, and stories may be developed and changed at will, as the situation and the child's imagination invite.

There are several kinds of plays without words, and these will appeal to children who have become old enough to separate action from conversation. *Statue posing* is the simplest (a boy is asked to stand in the attitude of the repentant publican of Jesus' story—then another, and another). *Picture posing* may be as simple as the addition of other statues (the Pharisee beside the publican, and perhaps the whole marketplace) or as complex as the recreation in costume and make-up of the painting of The Last Supper, or a series of pictures in a Christmas pageant. *Pantomime* adds action to posing, but still without words (the disciples gather, listen, eat, and depart). And *interpretive dance* stylizes the movement of pantomime (the Lord's Prayer or a Psalm of Praise is interpreted in symbolic movements by one or several participants). High school young people have found dance pantomime especially productive.

Story-playing adds words to pantomime. The words may be read by a narrator and the movements performed by silent actors. Or the actors may speak their own lines. The story may be a single scene or a narrative of epic proportions. *Puppets* may be substituted for visible actors, a method that often frees the puppeteer for remarkably imaginative speech and movement. Junior-age children are usually fascinated by this inside-outside relationship to the story. In the technique called *role-playing,* the situation is described and individuals play out the situation as they feel it, the "play" is discussed and evaluated, and then it is repeated with different actors and the different conclusion and characters are discussed. This technique is often used in parent and adolescent groups.

Dramatic forms may be used by the teacher to create *illustrated lessons* or by the minister to produce *illustrated sermons*. The reading of biblical narratives may be dramatized by assigning roles to various voices, and of the Psalms by grouping voices in *choral speaking*. This sort of reading is especially meaningful to older children and adolescents. Adults often find *play-reading* an interesting educational technique. The plays are read aloud without action or special costumes and later discussed; sometimes play scripts may be selected and programmed to form the curriculum for the study of problems and concepts. *Worship services* are sometimes dramatized, with the leaders and people participating in the acts of gathering, entering, offering, partaking, and dispersing, and in the speaking of prayer, praise, and thanksgiving.

Sometimes church groups combine various forms of creative dramatics for the celebration of special events in Christmas and historical *pageants*. And from time to time churches may go into full-scale *play-production*. The making of plays, however, is another subject entirely and beyond the realm of creative dramatics.

* * * * *

It is essential that, in undertaking the use of dramatic forms in the teaching-and-learning process, the procedure be such as to keep the emphasis squarely on the creative aspects of the project.

First, the story or situation is selected by the group itself. It should come as an outgrowth of the regular group study, and the teacher may exercise some influence by sensing the moment when the class is ready to turn study into story.

Then the story is divided into episodes or scenes, and these are discussed, selected, and arranged. This, too, is a group activity and not merely a product of the teacher's private analysis. Now the characters are studied as people, with a view to understanding and appreciating them. There will be more discussion, but there may also be considerable research. The time will come, then, when the group will be ready to choose which learners will play which characters. At this stage, the teacher will probably need to insist that the casting be kept fluid and perhaps even changed with every playing.

There are also decisions of a more technical sort to be made, and that may be accomplished as the above steps are worked through, or later as a separate matter. Costumes and properties will be discussed and designed. Ordinarily the teacher will try to keep these as simple as possible, but if it is the desire of the group to go into these matters, he will guide them toward authenticity, research, and function so that their development may itself be a learning process. Determining the place and scene will be the same kind of project. Task groups may be formed.

Meanwhile, the whole group will be repeatedly playing the story through, analyzing and evaluating, refining and correcting. Characters will be changed. Lines will be caught and polished. Movements will be simplified and clarified. The story will be perfected. It may sometimes be shared with another group which has an interest in the same subject matter. Over and over and over—until the teacher and the group sense that the learning process has reached its fulfillment. Then the group will move to some new subject or different method of learning.

*

Christianity is from first to last and from top to bottom a real drama characterized by the actual interaction of divine and human.

It is the purpose of the teacher of Christianity to enable learners to believe in and experience that drama for themselves. Imaginative reproduction in words and movement of memorable scenes from the divine-human drama will put learners on the same side of experience as the prophets, saints, and martyrs. Creative use of drama as a tool of exploration can help learners know how to risk the leap of faith. To stand beside a learner in that movement is both the method and reward of the teacher.

15

Worship

Worship is the divine-human dialogue brought to awareness.

Worship is not a method of teaching the lesson, but the lesson itself. Teaching Christianity is a humble but planned effort by the teacher to enable learners to explore and practice the meanings and dimensions of dialogue between learners and between the learner and the teacher. The purpose of practicing this horizontal dialogue is to illustrate and enable human response to the divine address. When man is aware of the divine-human dialogue, he is worshiping. In the teaching of Christianity, every session should come to the consciousness of the reality and presence of God, and whether it comes at the beginning, in the middle, or at the end of the lesson, whether it be acknowledged formally or informally, worship is the hoped-for and expected climax. Worship is thus the inevitable result of effective religious teaching. Nevertheless, all people constantly need specific, practical help in worshiping, and the teacher of Christianity must do what he can to help his learners to learn and practice the arts of worshiping. Bringing to awareness the dialogue that is actually going on is one of the special crafts of the teacher, but so also is helping to provide the means of recognizing and celebrating that wonder. Thus, worship is an exercise of the human response to the divine address that is both a function of the teaching-and-learning process in Christianity and a sign that the process has reached its intent.

*

Christian people worship. It is one of the most significant and distinctive things they do. They always have, of course—in private homes, catacombs, basilicas, cathedrals, village churches, log cabins, fox holes, and sleek A-framed, glass-sided air-conditioned edifices. They worship in many different ways—kneeling, standing, and sitting; in Latin, English, and "tongues"; formally, informally, and spontaneously. From this long and varied practice have emerged three conditions common to Christian worship: conviction, celebration, and community.

For Christians, worship proceeds from an experiential conviction about the nature of God and his relation to man. It is, therefore, a theological phenomenon and involves an objective content. Worship is an affirmation by the worshiper that God has done something for man that man cannot possibly do for himself, namely to address him in his human selfhood and selfishness with a call to reorient himself to the Other Person and to all other persons. It is an affirmation that God has made man for himself and that man is restless and unproductive until he finds his peace and destiny in response to God. Worship is constituted by such convictions as these and consists of their affirmation.

The man who has discovered this about God and himself is overwhelmed by a miracle of deliverance, and he glorifies and thanks God for it, simultaneously crying out in agony of spirit because he has at times made it seem incredible and therefore denied it. To do that is to burst the ordinary restraints of human indifference and diffidence and pour out words and acts of celebration. "Man's chief end is to glorify God and to enjoy him forever." This suggests that all men, children as well as adults, were made to worship, and that in worship as well as in life it is not man's nature to be entertained but to celebrate.

Indeed, this joy is so natural and so impelling that it must be shared. One heart alone cannot hold it. Each Christian simultaneously needs others and seeks to share with them. This sharing of God and man holds life together, and, together, bowing before the one God and Father of them all, drawing upon and supporting each other in their spiritual battles and victories, individuals become a community. It is a community of the same sort that the teacher of Christianity has been attempting to enable, session by session. Like teaching-and-learning, worship is not simply a personal matter, but also an event in which the individual voluntarily submits himself to the cooperative discipline of shared human response to the reality of God.

All these—conviction, celebration, community—can be talked about, practiced, nurtured. To do so will not necessarily conjure up the experience of worship but will provide and cultivate the circumstances out of which worship springs.

*   *

Worshiping has produced a combination of words, symbols, and acts. Yemenite Jews worship, shoeless and cross-legged, on the floor of their synagogue in Jerusalem, reciting their Torah. Moslems pray five times each day, prostrating themselves toward Mecca. Brahmin holy men worship in the silence they have kept unbroken for five years in mud huts beside the Ganges. Zen monks sit immovable for twenty hours a day in Kyoto, seeking to plumb the Buddha nature at the center of their being. The worshiping of Christians has created its own and distinctive forms.

In the Christian faith, worship is an occasion for the use and remembering of words. The Bible is publicly read and considered as a reminder of and instruction in God's revelation. The Word of divine address to men, the living *logos* that precipitated and penetrated the acts of patriarchs, prophets, and apostles and concreted itself in the Christ event, has through the centuries given rise to many words. Any serious discussion of the words—the tradition and content—of the Christian faith should be characterized by the essence if not the forms of worship. But further, it is the responsibility of the teachers and learners of Christianity to assist the Word to become meaningful not only to all the classes and conditions of men, but also to all the resistances and resources of youth, to all the ages and stages of children. Teachers and learners together will be constantly experimenting with the words of the dialogue in the effort to find new combinations that will be useful and meaningful in worship. They will, therefore, use in their worship the free verse paraphrase of the Lord's Prayer they wrote themselves, the dialogue version of the Apostles' Creed, and the hip-talk, off-beat form of the Sermon on the Mount that so interested them in class.

Through the centuries, Christian worship has produced a rich heritage of symbols in music, stained glass, sculpture, and painting, an architecture of special functions and forms. Protestant churches have tended to concentrate on music as their own special art form and have created an extensive and often inspiring literature of choral and congregational music. Some subtle and some massive ways of incorporating the crossed lines of the central Christian symbol into buildings have been designed, but Protestants have generally eschewed painting, and sculpture as idolatrous and even been chary of the use of stained glass. There have been some signs that a new alliance between the arts and faith is in the making, and a new and free symbolism comparable to the achievements of the medieval period may be in the offing. Meanwhile, teachers and learners in the Christian community should be constantly producing and sharing their own symbols for their own use in celebrating their awareness of the divine-human dialogue. Their own triptychs and murals for the worship center, their own music for new songs of praise, their own visions of the cross will be sought and used in worship.

The celebration of worship has also created liturgy and ritual, and Christians have found great meaning in the acts of kneeling, standing, walking, singing, offering their money, and praying together. For most Christians, the central act of worship is the ceremonial reenactment of Jesus' last meal with his disciples. For centuries, no matter how sacramental or symbolic their view of it may have been, Christians have known God most directly at the Table where they are drawn into Christ's sacrifice, victory, and way of life. Recently, liturgical revivals in Protestant churches have sought for fresh ways of acting out awareness of the divine-human dialogue in worship services. Teachers and learners in classes should be experimenting with liturgical forms of their own making as the experience of teaching-and-learning provides them: the liturgy celebrating the nativity of Jesus they composed, the new way they devised of collecting and offering their money, their own ways of entering and leaving the place of worship. A tip-toe processional of seven-year-olds may be more effective than the adult choir's sedate saunter, and it is quite possible that teen-agers may find sitting cross-legged on the floor in a circle to be a more meaningful presentation of themselves for worship than perching in mechanical rows on hard benches staring at the back of the girl in the next pew ahead.

* * *

In the teaching-and-learning process, worship experiences may be of three kinds—spontaneous, formal, and private—and the teacher of Christianity will attempt to nurture them all.

The essence of the worship experience should be arising constantly from the teaching-and-learning process itself. Whenever children are stirred by the experience of working together, or adolescents are seized by the meaningfulness of an ancient Christian doctrine, or adults plunge into a project for racial integration, the actual experience of worship may be ready to emerge into expression. It is then the responsibility of the teacher of Christianity to crystallize into overt words and acts what is already present. The teacher will always be trying, whether he is lecturing about the content of Christian beliefs, or illustrating the divine-human encounter in stories, or leading the learners in the give and take of discussion, to open the doors of the mind and spirit to the fact that God is here and now addressing each of them in love and enabling a reply. A word may be all that is necessary. There need be no liturgies or hymn singing, although on some occasions such an act may be meaningful. The moment may simply be one of silent awareness before the discussion moves on to the next issue. It is always the teacher's business to be yearning for the unbidden breakthrough to reality, his responsibility to be ready to draw aside the curtain of preoccupation and reveal the presence of the Spirit.

Formal worship should also characterize the teaching-and-learning of Christianity, and the teacher will find himself both arranging events and instructing in their practice. These services of worship may be frequent or infrequent, but they should probably be somewhat regular. They may be traditional or original, but they will probably be characterized by dignity rather than by form. They may be simple or elaborate, but they will be the result of careful planning. It is the teacher's responsibility to provide the learners with the necessary materials for worshiping. He may thus be called upon, with children, to teach hymns and prayers, or with any class, to encourage their creation. He will also find it necessary to assist with the preparation of the sequence of events or "order of worship," and perhaps to teach the learners how to prepare it themselves. He will find opportunities in the selection of hymns, the choice and performance of the scripture readings, and in the establishment of a propriety and unity in the materials for teaching. He will make it natural for everyone to contribute, if not in leading and reading and singing, then in creating the worship center or receiving the offering. He will seek ways to help his learners discover the meaning and use of silence. In teaching the preparation and conduct of formal worship, he will be helping to equip his learners with skills and materials that are meaningful not only now but will be useful throughout their lives. Teaching how to worship is one of the most precious and most often missed of the opportunities of the teacher of Christianity.

Private devotion and prayer has always been one of the characteristics of the Christian way of living; when it is not, the reason usually is that no training has been received. Exhortations and examples may be enough to inspire a courageous start, but the saints and mystics bear witness that it is continuous discipline that gives sustenance to daily life. They also make it very clear that they have found ways to do it that will be helpful to others. The best instructors in the geography of private prayer are these who have lived in that country. The teaching of Christianity should include the help they have to give in books or in person. It is also necessary to provide materials for individual use. They are of many kinds and of various sorts of appeal. A study of a broad spectrum of them is sometimes a very good course for young adults, and in a less formal way, the teacher may be constantly exposing his learners to them. Guided practice is also necessary, and the classroom provides many opportunities for practicing the discipline of silent meditation and reading. This sort of training is effective with older children, and should be practiced for far more reason than to achieve a respite for the teacher's tense nerves.

*

Overt acts of worship, combining and vivifying words and symbols, bring to life the dialogue of God's address to man and man's responses. Worship is not a withdrawal from life or from the teaching-and-learning process. It is a revitalization of life and the hoped-for accompaniment of learning experiences. It is the use of material things for spiritual purposes, a breaking into awareness of the divine-human dialogue. Worship is in both spirit and reality. It is a plunge into depth, a focusing of power. It will be a constant factor in all the ways of teaching-and-learning Christianity. It is the goal of the teacher, the ground of the process, and the heartbeat of the learner's own Christian life.

16

Discipline

Dialogue both limits and supports freedom.

There are two essentially different concepts of discipline, though devotees of both will agree that teaching-and-learning cannot proceed without some degree of it. On the one side are those who feel that control of the classroom depends primarily upon the teacher.

It is his responsibility, they say, to command respect from the learners and establish authority for his leadership. On the other side are those who feel that in the classroom control springs primarily from the learners. They believe that individual self-control comes into being in a setting of freedom.

There are many examples of the difficulties that arise when either concept is practiced in an exaggerated fashion. When the teacher-centered form of control is overdone, the demand for respect passes into rigidity and the insistence on authority soon becomes an arbitrary requirement for behavioral conformity. It almost seems that a spring is wound more and more tightly until, always unexpectedly, it snaps and shatters the whole mechanism. Teacher-tyranny was once almost the rule, it seems. Dotheboys Hall, as described by Dickens in *Nicholas Nickleby,* was a real horror chamber of resentment and hatred between teacher and learners. Old Boys from England's famed Public Schools still tell bitter tales of mistakes in Latin translation paid for in pain and tears. The rule of the rod in classrooms is largely a thing of the past, but there are still many teachers who insist on authoritarian control of the learners and the teaching process. Learner tyranny, judging from the reports of critics of American schools, now seems to be the general practice. In a chaos of immature self-rule, pupils have no respect for authority. They seem to do what they want to do until one day, according to the classic story, a pupil asks, "But *must* we do what we want to do today?" In slum schools, switch blades are sometimes pulled on the teacher who crosses the student. More usually, however, the tyranny is exercised by suburban, permissively raised children of upper middle-class parents who want to, and will, talk about baseball and movies rather than Esau and Jacob. There may be no tension, but eventually the class breaks down into incoherence and self-indulgence, and at last the time comes when there are no learners because none of them has bothered to come. Absolute permissiveness in classrooms probably does not exist as it once did, but there are still many teachers who insist that noncontrol is better than teacher control and that it is preferable for learners to develop their own interests and content as they go.

In contrast to both of these concepts of discipline is the concept of education as the enabling of dialogue. In this view, the primary purpose of teaching-and-learning is the establishment of a relationship between individuals which models the possibilities of divine-human interaction. When content is studied, it is for the purpose of illustrating and making credible that possibility in human life. The focus is therefore upon the persons and their relationships. Dialogue presupposes individuals; the chasms between them are so real that they cannot be closed but must be bridged. Each individual limits the freedom of each of the other individuals. There would be no meaningful freedom, however, were individuals not together, only independence and isolation. Further, the freedom not to respond to any address, human or divine, is essential for there to be any response. Dialogue thus both limits and supports freedom. The classroom where this meeting of persons in the presence of God is taking place will probably not be characterized by the stillness of the graveyard or the discipline of the army. There may be talking, laughing, and the sounds of making things. When content is studied, it will be the kind that invites overt dialogue. Neither the teacher nor the learner dominates the scene. They are all guided by their common purpose. Discipline is no longer a matter of who will exercise control, but a matter of what can be accomplished.

Resistance, both between individuals and to the content matter, is therefore thought of as a natural and necessary element of the teaching-and-learning process. It is invigorating for both the teacher and the learners. It raises the interest of both in the content. It reflects importance upon the events, both social and political, of the classroom. But, of course, resistance is not always healthy. It can turn into hostility or into indifference. Either will destroy the most precious gift the teacher has to offer the learners. Thus, when there is a serious dislocation of relationship, when one of the learners is sulking and yawning, when a learner makes it evident that he hates the class and the teacher, the situation cannot be allowed to continue. For it to do so not only invites disaster, it is also a blasphemy. This dislocation probably represents the greatest single difficulty to the teacher of Christianity.

In the moment of breakdown, there is probably only one rule: discipline is considered after the class session is over. When the class is in progress, there is too much to be thinking about for the teacher to make wise decisions about the offender and what to do. One of the universal lessons teachers learn sooner or later is that preoccupation on the part of the teacher with a question of discipline will almost certainly produce a discipline problem for the entire class. The reason for this is obscure. Mind reading hardly seems an adequate answer but may be as good as any. In some real way, the teacher's problem about discipline telegraphs itself to all the learners. Practically the only solution almost always is to get through the rest of the session, even at the cost of discarding the agenda outlined in the lesson plan, without a breakdown of personal relation between the teacher and the learners. After the session, the discipline problem becomes the first order of concern, to be thought through and planned for before the next session. Discipline can then be dealt with in terms of principle rather than of emotion.

*

Discipline in the teaching-and-learning process is built of a combination of several elements. Faced with a problem, or even with misgivings, the teacher should consider them. Such a review may reveal specific failures to the teacher. It is well to face them. The underlying purpose, however, is to assist in building a whole context in which freedom is both limited and supported.

The first and most personal element of discipline in the teaching-and-learning situation is the teacher's own self-discipline. Through the ages, whatever the cultural fashions in classroom management, the better teachers have used very little external compulsion upon their students. It is the inferior teacher, usually, who flogs and drives and roars. It is the teacher who exercises no discipline on himself who lets the children tear the place apart or permits the adult discussion to wander into total irrelevance. Teachers who know their subjects so well that they talk about them with interest and enthusiasm almost always fascinate their students: there are simply no empty spaces in time or interest for discipline problems to fill. And, even if the teacher is not inherently interesting, there is a massive integrity about the teacher who does not ask his pupils to do what he is not willing himself to do that generates real respect. Most teachers who really put time on their own preparation need not worry about controlling the pupils. Time spent worrying about discipline problems is often wasted; time devoted to disciplined preparation for the session is seldom lost in the session. Self-discipline inspires self-discipline.

Group responsibility is an important element in maintaining discipline. When the group has chosen its own goal, it is usually interested in accomplishing it. Discipline lags when nobody really understands why he is there. Purpose itself disciplines. It is remarkable how forceful a working group can be in dealing with one who interferes with or delays the work. Group controls should not be used as gimmicks for achieving discipline, but they can usually be counted on to work to that end when allowed to work in accord with their own nature. It is also noteworthy how gracefully the obstructionist will usually accept group will. With adolescents especially, but also with children and adults, the teacher can count on democratic self-discipline to establish and keep control of the group. In addition to dealing with the problem person, it will tend to keep the group from digression and from quitting before accomplishment. Let the group choose its own officers and set up its own rules and procedures. The teacher can lead the learners in believing that they will hit upon the right ways of working together, limiting discussion, and giving everyone a chance to make his own contribution. The teacher can also count on the operation of social pressures for help. Learners are part of a culture, ingroup and exclusive though it may be, in which there are some things that are done and others that are not. Sometimes they may seem strange to the teacher, but he can use their pressure in the group if he will but understand and trust them.

A healthy regard for facts and real things is an important element in the teaching-and-learning process, and it exercises an objective control over the classroom when it has been established. Facing facts frankly, admitting their reality, and acknowledging their limitations on human behavior is both a learning and a disciplining process. If a learner tries to bend window glass with a hammer, the nature of the glass exercises its discipline upon him. If a learner flaunts the offer of dialogue, he often becomes aware of an increasing incapacity for relationships of any kind. To do any sort of justice to the learning process itself, the teacher will be continuously attempting to establish the independence and validity of objective things. In so doing, he will be supporting discipline in the classroom.

Failure is a strong force in the development of discipline; a healthy regard for it should be built into the teaching-and-learning process. The inability to come to a conclusion in a discussion group cannot be permitted to immobilize the group, nor should it be passed over or ignored. It is usually an indication that some step has not been completed, some facts overlooked and a signal for review and refinement of the thinking process. Sometimes failure must be accepted and enclosed by the loving arms of the teaching-and-learning relationship. Indeed, there may be no factor more powerful, on occasion, in the building of discipline than living with real and unredeemable failure. Sometimes, even the total breakdown of discipline may be a failure productive of dialogue.

The goal of the teacher in building discipline, as in the enabling of dialogue, is to do his part and disappear. He must make his position known, but he must also make it clear that he is more interested in truth than in communicating his own ideas or maintaining his own importance. He is neither a propagandist nor a dictator, but a teacher. He must learn to be a leader so self-disciplined that he is able to stand aside in the quest for dialogue. His goal is the diminution of his own control to the vanishing point as the possibility of dialogue takes center stage.

By concentrating on building these elements into the teaching-and-learning process, the teacher will be both supporting and limiting freedom. More important, he will be building realism into dialogue.

*   *

Sometimes, however, discipline cannot be built and the problem thrusts itself into the open. Teacher and learner collide head on, from mutually exclusive positions and with antithetical emotions. As he considers that moment, certain essential principles may guide the teacher's eventual action.

Vengeance is impossible in the teaching of Christianity. Every art form has certain limitations, and this is one of the limitations of the art of teaching Christianity. In the Old Testament, vengeance is said to belong exclusively to the Lord. Whether or not personal animosity is ever justifiable where dialogue is the ground of the educative process, there can be no simple expression of bitterness and hatred by the teacher. He may expect to feel frustrated and beaten at times. This is the risk of his calling. He cannot, however, "take it out" on the learner. It is his responsibility to settle his own emotions before dealing with the situation, though it is not necessary that he hide the fact that he has had them from the offender.

Before the problem learner is dealt with on the grounds of his offenses, he must be known, personally and individually, by the teacher. Even if the teacher already knows him well, there is now reason to suspect that he does not know him well enough. It is now the responsibility of the teacher to understand him, insofar as possible, in the light of his behavior. He may have what are for him very good reasons for what he is doing. Learning anything worthwhile is difficult. Some find it downright painful. It is always tiring. He may be simply overwhelmed, shamed, embarrassed. On the other hand, what he does in class may not be caused by the class situation at all. If the social situation or the learner's personal adjustment is pathological, the teacher may need to find special help. It is very likely, however, that all that is required is a little overt understanding. In any case, the teacher's quest for more knowledge of the learner will let the learner know that the teacher is interested in him.

The teacher must also make every effort to love the problem learner. Since there is already antagonism between them, this will require some special doing. A few pats on the shoulder will hardly be enough at this stage of their relationship. Authentic kindness is invariable in love. Further, love includes judgment, and it may be necessary to add reproof and the offer of guidance to kindness. This is very difficult, but the teacher is occasionally called upon to step across a very wide chasm and to stand over there beside an experience dead set against his own.

Finally, if the decision is to exercise some direct punishment at the next session in case the learner again disrupts the class, the teacher of Christianity should deliberately make it more moderate than he thinks the learner deserves. The price of grace is always high, but its redeeming quality is great. The purpose of punishment in the teaching of Christianity is always educative: it is for the purpose of enabling dialogue. Should the learner prove absolutely incorrigible, resisting the best the teacher can offer, let him be provided with a tutor in a room apart, until he can be told to return to the class or to stay away completely.

*

Discipline is essential to the teaching-and-learning process. However, the process builds discipline. The basis of both is the give and take of free address and response. It is not to be expected that the process will go always without resistance and misunderstanding. It is to be expected, however, that they become part of the process, too, and given a chance they will be effective in the enabling of divine-human dialogue.

17

Evaluation

Constant evaluation is a strategy for helping the enabler of dialogue to give his best to the learners.

No teaching can be considered adequate without continuous and rigorous evaluation. The same is true of the teaching of Christianity. In the secular schools, the need has led to systems of objective

155

examinations, like the New York State Regents' Examinations for high school students, or the Graduate Records Examinations for college graduates. It has produced programs of Supervising Teachers who observe and criticize the classroom teacher's work. It has developed a wide variety of grading schemes, ranging from letters and percentages to written analyses.

The evaluation of the teaching of Christianity, however, encounters special difficulties. Rigorous and frequent examination of content matter seems to place the emphasis in the wrong place: it implies that Christianity is mastered by memorizing dates and names. Programs of observation by nonprofessional supervisors have created great resentment among the volunteer teachers of church schools. There has also been the implication that effective teaching of Christianity is no more than sophisticated classroom management. Grading has never been very successful in church schools. In addition to the major problem of subjectivity, there is the question of the meaning of the grades: there is no universal system of promotion or failure and no diploma or degree to be earned as the ultimate reward for passing the intermediate steps. Some interesting suggestions have been made, from time to time, along all these lines, from designing examinations that will have some sort of real meaning for both teachers and learners, to proposing that the entire enterprise of Christian education be integrated into a program of such quality that it would be valid to give elementary and secondary diplomas in Christian knowledge, leading at last to valid academic degrees for laymen.

The real problem with all these proposals is not so much practical as theoretical. A system of examinations could be constructed and a Christian school system created. Many of the materials and facilities are, in fact, already at hand. Why, then, has it not already been done? Certainly not merely because of disinterest or laziness. The heart of the problem is to be found in the essential nature of the teaching-and-learning of Christianity: both the method and the goal of the process are to enable the mysterious and personal event of human response to the divine address. How may the teacher judge whether that intimate transaction has occurred? Shall he grade the student's participation in it A for excellent or C for average? How may the teacher know what part he has played in that holy encounter? How may he evaluate the function of the teaching-and-learning process in the establishment of dialogue? In all candor, the teacher must admit that he cannot know and cannot judge.

A common response by teachers to this matter, however naïve or sophisticated it may be, is a shrug of the shoulders. It is usually a comforting gesture. This being the nature of the case, it is not only impossible but presumptive as well for anyone to lay objective requirements on his performance, be they denominational executives, other teachers, learners, or even himself. Shall he, then, merely take a pious attitude toward his work and run the risk of lapsing into sloppy shenanigans on holy ground? Too often this seems to have been the result. Church school teachers are notorious for hoping that their work has been effective. Some even pray that it may be. They tend to remember that Johnny asked an interesting question week before last and leap to the conclusion that everything is as it should be, not only with John but with the whole class and, further, with their conduct of it.

Of course, there is nothing wrong with hope, prayer, and flashes of interest. Every teacher must, however, if he has any inkling of the momentous portent of his role as enabler of the divine-human dialogue, feel the imperative for being as effective an enabler as possible for those very real and needy learners in their concrete living and doing. Nothing less than his best is worth offering. He needs a discipline to keep his offer at its best. The most effective discipline is self-applied, but in order to avoid mere subjectivism in

157

evaluation, self-discipline must be regularly and vigorously practiced.

The first act of the teacher of Christianity after a class is to evaluate the session.

*

Though there are no objective guides that can give the teacher of Christianity an absolute sort of judgment about his effectiveness in the teaching-and-learning situation, there are a number of indirect evidences. None of them is to be taken as meaning much by itself. Together they may supply a judgment to be trusted.

Attendance and punctuality are guides to learners' interest, and the interest or disinterest of learners provides a preliminary insight into whether the teacher is meeting the learners in any significant way. Of course, it is always possible that Mary's regular attendance is merely habitual, and Jimmy's punctuality is due to parental discipline. In general, however, it is probably true that when pupils come regularly and on time, without the offer of ulterior rewards or the application of outside pressures, the class is meaningful to them. The reverse may also be assumed: when learners are frequently absent and late and there are no other clear reasons for this irregularity, it is probable that the class sessions are not important to them.

Once they are there, the attitudes of the learners in class to one another and to the teacher provide another general clue to educational effectiveness. Do they give the appearance of being interested? Do they seem to be responding wholeheartedly to the teacher's suggestions and ideas? Are they loyal to the group? In addition to these general attitudes in class, there are more objective evidences to be evaluated. When outside work is assigned, has it been done, and how? When there is recitation and discussion, do the learners seem to be understanding the material and taking it seriously? Are they relating their public school work, life on the job, and daily events to the subject matter of the class? The question-and-answer method of teaching practiced by Socrates was, in a sense, a continuous examination of learners by the teacher. It is a good way of teaching, sometimes. When it is practiced, it offers direct evidence about the quality of the learning.

The nature of the learners' worship times is also an indication of what is really going on in the teaching-and-learning process. If worship is the divine-human dialogue brought to awareness, the occurrence of spontaneous moments of worship in a class session is evidence that the teaching is reaching its mark. The formal worship periods in which the learners participate, either in the school or in the church, will also reflect what is happening in the class sessions. Is the learners' attitude reverent or bored? Do they participate in the worship service? Do they seem to understand what they are doing? Is there evidence of some appropriate satisfaction achieved in participating? The state of health of the learners' worship life may be taken as an indication of the state of the teaching-and-learning session.

The sort of relationship learners seem to have to the church may also be an indication of how the class is going for them. There being no special pressures applied, when learners attend church, take part in its activities, are loyal to it and join it, it may be concluded that the teaching-and-learning of Christianity has been effective. When they will have nothing else to do with the church's life apart from the class sessions, the teacher has a signal for further inquiry. Criticism of the church is always healthy, and adolescents and young adults sometimes seem to specialize in it. Abstention from the activities of the church is not necessarily unhealthy. It is all, however, data for rigorous evaluation.

The everyday life of the learners should reflect something of the classroom. This is the point at which the real breakdown of Christian teaching is most often visible: the eager young Christians of

Sunday morning show little evidence the rest of the week of actually understanding the lessons they had apparently thoroughly grasped in class. The connections between learning and living are tenuous and little understood. The forces of life are so complex that the teacher of Christianity cannot hold himself directly responsible for the daily paganism of his pupils. Nevertheless, daily life is the test of Christian teaching. The teacher must be willing to submit his work to this test and unwilling to explain away the negative results. He must be prepared to fail the test, and be determined to carry on more effectively. To do so, he must know his learners outside the class session. That will contribute both to his humility and to the effectiveness of his teaching.

A good teacher will constantly evaluate his work. These tests will provide some guidance in the practice of that discipline. The first thing he does after each session of the class is to review the period, taking note of specific comments and acts, building a more and more comprehensive picture of each learner. In this act of evaluation, the learners themselves seem to stand in judgment upon his teaching, and thus the teacher has once more practiced the essential discipline of the art of teaching Christianity—crossing to the other side of the learning experience.

*   *

The art of giving examinations is a problematical one. Examinations are said by some progressive educators to be a snare and delusion and by some traditional educators to be the stuff and staff of the educational process. Examinations are, however, widely used in secular schools, and almost universally by the teachers of objective subjects such as science, mathematics, and history. The memory of exhausted eyes, frayed nerves, and intolerable pressure is associated with them by learners, and of tedious reading, uncertain judgments, and overwhelming discouragement by most teachers. However, nobody has yet thought of a real substitute, and some educators seem currently to be fascinated with the possibility of transforming the whole process of examination taking and giving into a machine-like business in which the learner punches holes in cards and the teacher runs the punched cards through a computer. Everybody knows that when the teacher gives an examination the learners take out gems of knowledge, polish them up, and display them. When the examination is over, they put them away or throw them away. Facts on file are not worth very much in themselves, but that is precisely what objective examinations reveal.

In the teaching-and-learning of Christianity, examinations have their place, so long as the essentially objective and fact-repeating nature of examinations is understood and remembered. There is no reason that ten-year-olds studying the Joseph epic, or high school students learning of the fourth-mentury doctrinal controversies, or adults surveying the history of the Old Testament, should not be encouraged to discover whether or not they have memorized the basic facts. True-false, multiple choice, and completion type tests may be very useful in helping the teacher and the learners find out. More originality is required of the learner in the essay and problem centered examinations, and they are much more difficult for the teacher to evaluate. The teacher of Christianity who uses any of these forms should be willing to learn how to construct examinations that are clear, comprehensive, and challenging, and to spend a great deal of time and originality creating them and evaluating the returns. A good test is always an accomplishment and is usually also an effective teaching instrument. Asking the essential questions, suggesting new relationships between apparently discrete facts, prodding the learner to think for himself are the real goals of testing. To accomplish this requires a thorough knowledge of the subject matter by the teacher, and the capacity to see it from the learner's point of view. The teacher should also remember that students in recent years have had wide experience with examinations in the public schools and colleges and can identify a sloppily constructed test in thirty seconds of exposure to it.

There is a growing literature of subjective examinations which may be useful to the teacher of Christianity, especially if the subject matter of his classes deals with attitudes and values. If he is interested in this kind of instrument, the teacher will find help at colleges of education, denominational headquarters, and in textbooks on the theory of testing in the local school library. In reading the results of some of these tests, the teacher may learn more about the learners than he has taught them.

In the work of great teachers, however, it would appear that the best kind of examination has for centuries been oral. The written examination did not come into general use until the nineteenth century. In medieval universities the public disputation was the final examination, and a rigorous test it was, for the entire university and often the neighboring community came, and the candidate was subjected to interrogation from all points of view, ranging from the town butcher to the student's major professor. If he was a good student, the examination was likely to end in public controversy. And if he was a brilliant student, he won his right to be a teacher of teachers. Oral examinations may be formal: the learner is given an appointment of an hour or two with his teacher and perhaps other specialists. No questions are out of bounds, and the learner is strictly on his own mettle. Oral examinations may be informal: the teacher is constantly pressing questions upon the learner during the class session. Teachers of Christianity could well make more use of both forms. The oral examination has the merit of preserving the actual form of dialogue, and should, therefore, become a teaching-and-learning situation as well as an occasion for learner reporting. A modified revival of the medieval disputation could be an exciting thing in the life of a church. It could be practiced at year's end in the high school years on a one to one basis, for in most classes there are not more than a dozen or fifteen learners to one teacher. It could be developed for applicants for church membership, with an appointed examining board. It could be applied to candidates for the teaching faculty of the church school, in which the new faculty demonstrate their right to teach. In these cases, of course, the community of believers and teachers owes the learner both an adequate preparation and a rigorous examination.

* * *

Programs of observation have as their goal the improvement of teaching by subjecting the performance of a teacher with his learners to the evaluation of a third party. This is sometimes a traumatic experience for the observed teacher. It is never an easy task for the observer, who becomes not only an intruder upon the teaching-and-learning situation but also a judge of another teacher's work. It is often worth the risks, however, for no matter how conscientiously the teacher may evaluate his own teaching, his will always be a personally involved and subjective judgment. If observation is to be used as a method of evaluation, it must be done carefully, by teachers who themselves have been teachers, and for the specific purpose of developing and encouraging the observed teacher. It has the merit of helping the teacher-of-learners to cross over the chasm of experience and become, now and again, a learner-of-teachers.

The basic procedure is simple, and the possible outcomes are multiple. A class session is visited by an observer upon appointment and with the consent of the teacher. It is essential to preserve the integrity of the teacher and his authority in his own classroom. After the observation, there will be a teacher-and-observer conference. It should be soon, unhurried, and proceed upon the basis of written notes. It is not the primary responsibility of the observer to criticize or to compliment, but rather to reflect what happened in the classroom. Together, in a teaching-and-learning relationship, teacher and observer may review the actual events of the session. The teacher is encouraged to see his work from the observer's side of experience, in order to help him understand the learner's side. Upon the basis of this conference, many different plans of action for the improvement of the teacher's work may be developed. They may decide upon a course of reading and study, either in the field of the content or of teaching methods. They may begin a program of visitation in the homes of the learners. They may inaugurate a plan for redecorating or reequipping the classroom. They may arrange for the teacher to be relieved for a period so that he may observe other classes. They may agree to shift the teacher to another class or to different material.

Whatever is decided will be mutually agreed. The purpose of observation is the further enabling of dialogue. It is a teaching-and-learning process, also. By involving the teacher in address-and-response concerning his own work, it is brought to mutual judgment and cooperatively improved.

*   *   *   *

The work of every class may also be submitted to the entire community of teachers and learners for occasional review and evaluation. This is not so much a trial on the one hand, or demonstration on the other, as a program of sharing with everyone the teaching-and-learning experiences. As a result, performance is evaluated and good performance supported.

The attendance charts sometimes kept by church schools are one form of this sharing but are usually neither very important nor revealing. More significant would be exhibits of work done in the class: the maps, time lines, models, and mosaics. Some classes would be able to display books and resources: a collection of Bibles, pictures from overseas missions, artifacts from medieval Europe. A central place in the building could be provided, or display cases outside each room. Occasionally, classes can present programs for others to attend: plays, music, or demonstrations. The work of learners may find expression in worship services: reading, worship centers, original hymns, and prayers.

These sharing projects must, of course, be kept in hand. It is possible to imagine a situation in which the work in classes is devoted for weeks to preparing something spectacular to show. The only motive may be the teacher's aggrandizement. Public school teachers have learned to dread Parent nights and PTA visitations. That which is shared must be the honest outgrowth of actual classwork, and the sharing itself a mere incident in the overall teaching-and-learning process. However, sharing is an essential element of the Christian life, and the offering of one's discoveries to one's brothers is an address inviting response.

*

Evaluation may be of the nature of dialogue. Inasmuch as it is, a teacher's self-criticism, the giving and taking of examinations, the observation of a teacher's work, and the sharing of results of the teaching-and-learning process are all enablers of address and response. Evaluation is therefore a teaching method which takes place outside of class. It begins the moment the class session has ended, and extends the teacher's learning into his own life. It enables the teacher to give of his best to his learners.

18

Teaching the Bible

To teach the Bible is to expose learners to sacred events resulting from dialogue between God and man.

For the teacher of Christianity, there is no question whether the Bible is to be taught. The only question is how it can be done best, and the teacher will always be on the alert for methods and materials that improve his teaching of it. The Bible will be taught both specifically and incidentally. It will be the subject of special courses, in which the teaching-and-learning method will range from lecturing to group activities. It will be investigated both generally in survey form and in depth in studies of selected parts. The purpose of this teaching will be to give the learners, by the time they have finished high school, a thorough grasp of the literature, the history, and the religion of the Jews and early Christians. It will also flow constantly into lessons on other subjects, from church history to contemporary social problems. The purpose of this teaching will be to assist the learners to discover how the biblical experiences and wisdom can be put to work throughout life.

The Bible will be taught in the conviction that included in its pages is an ancient sacred history still at work. From a vast store of the experiences of a people peculiarly sensitive to the divine address, certain episodes have been selected, worked over and tied together for the purpose of presenting a record of the relationship between God and man. Some of it is factual and some of it is mythical. It is important, wherever possible, to distinguish between them and to identify the work of various writers and editors. All the episodes and themes and threads, however, add up to a whole greater than all of its elements: it is a body of material so effectively embodying the intent of God that God mysteriously speaks through it to the reader. In one degree or another, in many different languages and logics, this has been the universal witness of Christian history: in the Bible, both old and new sections, men meet God at work, yearning and acting for their salvation. The purpose of teaching this material will be to expose learners to the possibility of divine-human dialogue in their own experience.

*

The Bible may be taught and learned as event and episode. A large part of it is made up of stories about people with peculiarities, strengths, and weaknesses that render them essentially credible and interesting. The drama tends to run high, sometimes to the melodramatic, for its content is action rather than conversation. Deeds rather than words are the stuff of the biblical view of life. There are funny stories and sad stories. There are accounts of astounding human greatness and poignant smallness. There are epics (serialized stories that run on and on with one character at the heart of them all) and episodes (single vignettes that catch in a paragraph the essence of an event or personality). There are military yarns and domestic tales, stories of frontier life and of royal courts.

All of them are worthwhile simply as stories, and ought to be known and treasured by Christian folk. The secret lies in telling them well as rightful accounts of human behavior. Most of them are so well constructed that they should be read, rather than retold by anyone but a good storyteller. Let there be no pious intoning of the words because they happen to be from the Bible, but rather let them be told and read with the zest for detail and craftsmanship any well-told story deserves. Especially should Christians hear the Gospels read out loud; a reading of the Gospel of Mark takes no longer than an average evening in the theater, and almost no one has ever heard the whole story of his Lord recited at once. Every church school should encourage some person with the gift and technique for reading well to become the school's master reader of Bible stories, and he should be kept at work regularly. They should be heard for fun, for entertainment, for worship, for instruction— for no special reason at all—until everyone knows and loves them. This experience will begin, of course, in early childhood. It will last throughout life.

*   *

The Bible may also be taught and learned for its sounds and cadences. No purer diction may be heard in the English language than the Bible in a serious translation, from the King James Version to the J. B. Phillips paraphrases, and the same may be said of German in the Martin Luther translation. Poems, dramas, sermons, and epistles ring with the actual sounds of beauty, passion, aspiration, love, and hope. The meaning of the words is literally enhanced and extended by the sheer sound of the words.

Now that modern poetry has broken the shackles of mere grammatical style forced upon it by the Age of Rationalism, it is no longer thought to be mystical or sensuous to hear sounds and meanings together; the Bible excels in this ancient yet modern form of writing, and should be heard read aloud by skilled readers sensitive to the meaning of Scripture. Some professional actors have sensed this need and have recorded passages of their own choice; they tend to be histrionic and artificial because the actor's understanding has lagged behind his craft, and he has sought to make up with flourish what he knew he lacked in grasp. Many ministers do not read the Bible well because their understanding has outrun their craft, and they tend to insinuate a false piety into their reading because they know their technique is not up to the meaning of the material.

There are people, however, perhaps because they are unaware of the problems overwhelming actors and ministers, who do read the Bible simply, directly, and meaningfully. They should be put to work reading it aloud for everyone to hear, and not only on worship occasions. Many are the people of various stations and achievements who have given credit for both their wisdom and their diction to hearing the Bible read from childhood in the family circle. And there are many more for whom the entire Bible has been spoiled and made irrelevant by hearing it read only in halting mispronunciations and stumbling misinterpretations by unskilled peers as they read around the circle verse by verse. The experience of hearing the nonnarrative parts of the Bible read well and often may begin with middle childhood. It never loses its interest.

169

*   *   *

The Bible may also be taught and learned as literature. It is literally a library, important because of its content, its antiquity, and its quality. The same sort of analytical appreciation should be brought to it that is exercised upon any documents of importance. These skills and how to teach them to learners are described in every good textbook on literature. The major questions of literary analysis should be applied to each unit of the biblical material and may be pressed without insecurity: the Bible will not stand or fall, even for them, because of negative literary decisions reached by a class. *What was the writer trying to say?* The answer comes at several levels: his message as a whole, summarized, if possible, in a single thesis sentence; his theme ideas, isolated and identified; his special concepts and concerns, whether they seem to be in direct logical support of the major thesis or not. *Has he said it?* A student of the document needs to decide how effective the statement has been, and be able to identify the elements that make the message communicate, if it does. There is a second decision: whether this student, himself, understands the message, and what it means to him. How does this compare with what the document seemed to mean when it was written? *How did the author say it?* The literary form should be identified and understood, whether it be poetry, drama, story, sermon, or letter. And the quality of the language should be savored, sentence by sentence. It is this part of the analysis that will probably take the most time in class, and bring about the most discussion. *Was it worth saying?* Was the message particular or universal? What effect did it have on its first readers? On those who have followed? What place does it occupy in the whole biblical collection?

This literary appreciation of the Bible may not begin before later childhood, and the process of building it may last a lifetime.

*   *   *   *

The Bible may also be taught and learned as history. Of course, the Bible is not a textbook of ancient history. It falls far short of modern scientific standards of historical evidence. It also goes far beyond any such standards in presenting the inside feeling of its own story and people. With some appreciation of the stories, the sounds, and the literature of the material in the background, the Bible may be freely studied and appreciated as a special sort of historical document. This process may begin with junior high school students, and it, too, may last a lifetime.

A comparison between the major, relatively historic events of the biblical story and documented nonbiblical events should be maintained at all times. A time line or chart will be a helpful aid. Of course, it will be necessary to rely on some biblical scholar for these data, and even so, the learners must be kept aware of the historical indefiniteness of many biblical events. A good textbook of Jewish history, of which there are a number published for various levels of readers, will be a handy companion, and might, at some time, provide the material for a separate course. Public school courses in ancient history should be taken into account, and perhaps a church school class in Old Testament history could be correlated with them.

The critical materials concerning individual writings will be collected and discussed. Is it possible to determine when the material was written? How does its date relate it to other biblical and nonbiblical documents? What are the collateral evidences? How much guessing is necessary to fix a date? How important is it to have a date or even a guess? What was the whole cultural situation? What was going on elsewhere? Does the document reflect the attitudes of the desert or of the town, of Palestine or the diaspora, of the kingdom or of the occupation? Who was the author? How near was he to the events he was describing? What collectors and editors have had their hands in reworking the material? Even if the author cannot be named and identified, what sort of man was he, judging from his work? To whom was the work written, spoken, or sung? What was their reaction to it? What attitudes does it reflect of the author and of the surrounding situation: that of the exclusivistic covenant community or a universalism, a national theology or an emergent monotheism, holistic Hebrew thought or analytical Greek wisdom?

The religious themes will be considered. What is the content of revelation—God's self-disclosure—in this writing? How is it conveyed? What did it mean then, and what does it mean now? How is God seen to be acting, and what are the responses of men, positive and negative? How does the major theme correlate with man's universal needs? To what "ultimate questions" does this writing provide an answer, and what is it? How does the material relate to the Christ Event and the meaning of Jesus for the Christians? If it is New Testament material, what does it say specifically about the nature of Jesus, the incarnation, the resurrection? What influence has it had on the development of the church and doctrine? How can it be used devotionally today? How does it serve to make clear the address of God to man and enable a positive response?

*　　*　　*　　*　　*

It is necessary to decide, as wisely as possible, in what sequence and at what ages to expose learners to these several approaches to teaching-and-learning the biblical content. A knowledge of both developmental psychology and the nature of the Bible is necessary, and many different theories have been developed. A consideration of the following proposal might lead to some decisions. When they have been made, it is important that they be carried through with sensitivity to the learners' needs and capacities and, at the same time, without leaving gaps in the overall coverage of the material.

From five to eight years of age, the concentration could be on Old Testament episodes and on daily life in the time of Jesus. From eight to eleven years, the need is for action, during which the biblical instruction could center on the sagas and epics, and on the whole life and death of Jesus. At the end of childhood, perhaps in the twelfth year, the prophets could be studied. The shift from action to literature can be accomplished in this year, beginning with the stories of the prophets and building to a literary appreciation of the prophetic books. In the years from thirteen to fifteen, all this material may be reviewed with a focus on historical study. These are the data-demanding years in the development of most young people. A broad sweep of the material and a detailed analysis of some parts can both be accomplished in three years. In the sixteenth through eighteenth years, when most young people become philosophers for the first time in their lives, the concentration can be on the biblical message, the religious and theological themes.

*

The questions of the nature of myth in regard to the Old Testament and how much the energetic propagandizing of the early Christians affected the historical authenticity of the New Testament record have loomed very large in scholarly debate in recent years. The approach outlined here has taken account of this debate and is proposed with a view to giving a growing Christian some ground for dealing with such questions. More important, however, is the fact that the purpose in teaching-and-learning the Bible is to expose learners at every stage of their development to an authentic experience of the divine-human dialogue on the frontiers of their own living. The Bible has long been known as a spectacularly adult book. By the time a Christian is eighteeen years of age, the Christian community owes him an adequate preparation for an adult study of the Bible.

19

Teaching History

To teach history is to expose learners to events precipitated by human response to the address of God.

Christianity is nothing if it is not a historical religion. Some other religions are not certain how seriously history should be taken. There is no doubt for the Christian, however, about that. History matters to Christians. It matters because it arose, at the beginning, out of certain events connected with the life, death, and resurrection of Jesus of Nazareth in Palestine. It matters because they understand the essence of these events to be continued through nineteen successive centuries of believing and disagreeing, living and dying, organizing and reforming by people who knew themselves to be his followers and agents. It matters, ultimately, because Christians hold that the eternal and infinite God acts in time and space among the lives of human beings. Man's life is real because he experiences it to be, and meaningful because God participates in it. These events are worth remembering, both because they are real and meaningful, and, in addition, because they enable man to plunge on into new and original events with trust and courage. It is therefore important that Christian people know about their historical tradition. In short, the history of Christianity must be taught.

There may be some scientific doubt about the specific authority of some events in the story of Christianity. Because history matters, the Christian often becomes a historian, seeking in documents and artifacts the "real truth" of the situation. Ordinarily, he is so much a historian that he is ready to accept the evidence, even if it throws doubt on events he had taken to be scientifically true. Further, there are wide differences about the meaning and the importance of some of the events of the Christian story. Because history matters, the Christian often becomes also a philosopher of history, using historical evidence as a means to finding universal truths. In fact, history matters so much to most Christians that they become propagandists for it. In short, they teach the history of Christianity.

Now, this enthusiasm for teaching history seems to go dead against two favorite beliefs of the modern secular mind. Contemporary street-corner man tends to prefer a world that is all foreground. He likes for everything that he must deal with to be "right out in the open" where he can see it, and for it to be very much what it

176

appears to be. Great heights, especially as regards ideas, and great distances, especially as regards time, tend to make him uncomfortable. He prefers the dominance of the present tense which tells him that everything that really matters is Now, and the provincialism that convinces him that what is really important is Here. Contemporary educators also appear to prefer a foreshortened world, combining John Dewey's world-in-constant-flux of pragmatism with John Doe's here-and-now world of practical-ism. This is something of a misinterpretation of John Dewey, who was a scholar as well as a critic of the history of ideas, whose philosophy made heavy use of massive "rhythms" and "cumulative progression," and whose educational program involved children in the exploration of the experiences of history for the purpose of guiding future experiments. And it is also something of a misinterpretation of John Doe, whose profound concern for the uncertain future reflects importance on past events, and whose life in a divided world forces him to be interested in different cultures with different histories, leaving him deeply distrustful of his own preference for a simple two-dimensional existence.

Man without history is therefore a disturbed, introverted, flattened creature. He needs a sense of depth and distance in order to exist in history. He also needs to know how God has worked in some events to restore and redeem them so that he may recognize the invitation of God in his own events. Both the distress and the needs of contemporary man are on the side of the teacher of Christian history.

*

History is a demanding subject to teach, partly due to the nature of the subject. It is worth working at.

In the first place, history is inclusive. It is a vast subject. It literally includes every event in the human past, the whole struggling, stumbling, strutting, serving, suffering, surviving, stunning story. It includes not only the important and the successful, whose stories are amply documented, but the failures and the misfits who were always there, though most of them are now nameless and forgotten. It includes the errors and illusions and stupidities as well as the truths and the insights and the wisdom. It includes all man's knowledge and ideas, at any given time and all together.

Obviously, all that cannot ever be learned or taught. It is, however, precisely the task of the teacher, as Martin Buber points out in a memorable passage, *to make a selection of the effective world*. It all "educates" the human being, drawing out his powers and making him grasp and penetrate its difficulties. The entire world engenders the person in the individual. All that is going on all the time. Education comes into being, however, when the teacher selects, consciously, from that mass of influences and gives decisive effective power to that which he has chosen by his decision and presentation. In this way, says Buber, through the educator the world becomes for the first time the true subject of its effect. The teacher of Christianity functions in the same way. He does not teach all of history, he selects the story of Western man. He does not present all of that, he chooses the story of Christianity in it. He does not deal with it all, he selects certain periods or themes which are meaningful for him and can be grasped by his learners. And he does not attempt to treat all of that, for he finds those occasions of man's response to or rejection of God's address which will give ground to stand on and body to stand with for the learner's own experience.

The teacher is called upon to make this selection partly as historian and partly as teacher. As historian, he is concerned that the materials chosen will provide at least a fair representation of the materials he has omitted. As teacher, he is concerned that the materials he chooses will be sufficiently within the experience and understanding of his learners to communicate to them and sufficiently new and exciting to them to stretch them.

History is also personal. It is not concerned with objective happenings, but with events as they become part of human experiences and affect them; it is concern with the world of nature and institutions, but only so far as they provide and limit the field of human activity and set the problems which men must solve. History is personal, not only because it deals with persons, but also because it recounts the divine-human dialogue which constitutes man a personal being. The teacher's task is therefore also personal, that is, not just to reconstruct the outline of actions, dates, and names, but to bring the past into memory. Remembering is an individual and private act. The teacher is engaged in the act of recalling and revivifying memories of the Christian movement, and placing them in the memory of learners who had not previously been aware that all this had happened to them. In the memory, these events become sources of action for the Christian movement. Some say that nothing experienced by a person is ever lost to his memory. This may also be true of a movement: it has been suggested that if, by some selective fire all the Bibles in the world were burned, it could be entirely reconstructed from the memory of those who know and love it. It is the responsibility of teachers of Christianity to fill the memory of living Christians with the historic tradition in which they participate.

*   *

In the teaching-and-learning of history, the teacher of Christianity is called upon, not to make the distant near, but to make the distant real and relevant. Doing that requires certain skills of the teacher and certain capacities of the learner.

The first requisite for the teaching-and-learning of history is a sense of before and after. Before they begin school, children develop a practical awareness that events occur in sequence, but a sense of the historical relation of cause and effect is built up slowly and painfully through punishment for misbehavior, the coming of measles after exposure, the requirement that play comes only after the dessert is finished. The concept of "historical trend" is one of the most elusive problems for both teachers and learners and is built on top of the sense of before and after and the awareness of cause and effect. The historian knows that all events relate to one another, and that it is impossible to have the Reformation without the Renaissance and the Middle Ages or the Dark Ages. But he also knows that if he had been himself living in the Renaissance, knowing it could not have been without the Middle Ages or the Dark Ages, he would probably have been unable to predict the Reformation. And he knows, also, as a modern historian, that even if he knew all about the Renaissance and the Middle Ages, he could not explain the forms and times and persons of the Reformation. It is the teacher's task, especially in telling the story of Christianity, to communicate the independence and interdependence of history along with the meaning of what it means to say that. It is the teacher's responsibility never to teach history without calling into play the learner's capacity to understand before and after.

Another requisite for the grasp of history is a sense of the length of time. For a small child, "tomorrow" is so distant as to be meaningless. "Next week" does not become meaningful much before middle childhood. It takes a dozen or more experiences with "a year" to have much idea of how long that is. To understand "a century" is necessarily an abstraction, since none of us actually lives one for himself. To project the amount of living and dying that comprises a millennium baffles most adults. Yet there are two millennia in the Christian story! Learners all need help in sensing what it means to talk about Luther four hundred years ago, St. Francis in the thirteenth century, and Augustine just before the fall of the Roman Empire. Still, history is meaningless without a sense of time. Residents of Europe, surrounded by buildings that are centuries old, and of the Orient, nurtured in the changelessness of customs and styles, tend to absorb this sense of time. The teacher of American children will need to seek out illustrations of age in the community and expose learners to them. A time line is an indispensable aid for all ages of learners. If an entire year is scaled to a mere inch, the line representing the Christian era will be 166 feet long! No historic event or person should be mentioned without placing him properly on the line and perhaps discussing before and after as well. Only with constant help can learners make the leap across to the other side of a century.

The capacity to cross over into another culture is also required if history is to be meaningful. Children are able to make this crossing much more easily than adults, which should furnish some clue not only as to when but also as to how it may best be done. Imagination is the key, and all the sense gates possible should be used in helping learners feel the historic culture from the inside: showing models and pictures; putting on clothing, eating food and role playing customs; telling stories and presenting movies; and finally but far from least in importance, reading the original sources in whatever translations or condensations may be necessary for understanding. There is a fabulously rich fund of pictures of buildings and paintings, recordings of plays and sermons and music from every period of Christian history. An astounding number of the "great books" of Christian history are available in paperback editions. The teacher has no excuse for not putting his learners into direct touch with significant primary sources. Both children and adults should be expected to participate in the whole spectrum of learning experiences, even children in reading sources and even adults in role-playing customs. An imaginative teacher can help learners build a bridge into past cultures.

Accuracy is essential in teaching and learning history. The teacher will become something of a scholar in his passion for getting the facts as straight as possible. When he does, learners will usually respond with a corresponding eagerness. Together they will play the all-important game of distinguishing between "weak facts" and "strong facts," record and interpretation. Any learner beyond the fifth grade enjoys it, and when he reaches junior high school, let the teacher beware of any temptation to do a sloppy job of research, for that is the age of incipient skepticism when only the facts matter. When the learners are of high school age, they will be more interested in interpretation than in facts, but they will be ready, also, to share the process by which the record is turned into judgments.

Learning the history of Christianity calls for the use of a complex of skills. It seems, however, that the complex is made up of parts that are developed naturally and can be drawn together accumulatively by skillful teachers. With instruction that makes use of these skills, the learning of history can be exciting.

* * *

The Christian tradition is a rich heritage. Every Christian deserves to possess the vivid and personal memory of at least a dozen fulcral episodes about which the intricate history of the Christian movement can be organized. He should have them all well in hand by the time he finishes high school. At various periods throughout his secular school career, he will be studying these same periods from a more general point of view; the alert teacher of Christianity may find opportunities for correlating his teaching of Christian history with his learners' weekday studies. There will be debate about any list of major episodes and writings in the history of Christianity; the following might precipitate dissent that could be worthwhile:

> The Martyrdom of Polycarp, together with some secondary
> sources;

The Nicene Council, with Eusebius and Athanasius as primary
    sources;

The *Pastoral Rule* of Gregory the Great;

The life and reign of Charlemagne;

The life and devotional writings of Bernard of Clairvaux;

The story of all the Crusades;

The contemporary "Lives" of Francis of Assisi;

The *Imitatio Christi* and the Brethren of the Common Life;

Martin Luther and the Reformation Treatises of 1520;

Roger Williams and the *Bloudy Tenent of Persecution;*

The life and many of the *Sermons* of John Wesley;

The letters and life of William Carey;

The life and some of the writings of Albert Schweitzer.

The primary sources for most of these episodes can be found in
paperback translations. The modern teacher of Christian history has
no excuse for not putting his learners to work on them.

*

There has been considerable debate among scholars as to whether
the historian should be primarily a scientist or an artist. The teacher
of Christianity will rely on the scholars for resources and guidance.
He will probably not be able to claim to be a scholar himself. But
when he teaches Christian history he may find himself to be a
scientist in his study of facts, an artist in his selection of material,
and a theologian in his interpretation of events. He will do his
best because history matters. He may not be a great teacher, but he
will take advantage of the naturally developing interests of his
learners and the teaching techniques available. It should then not be
unexpected if the teaching-and-learning of the history of the
Christian movement not only informs the learner but also invites
him to participate in the same dialogue which engaged great men
of long ago.

20

Teaching Theology

Theology is the attempt to represent the experience of divine-human dialogue in words. All teaching of Christianity is dealing with theology.

Whenever anything of any importance happens, it seems to be virtually a necessity for civilized man to find some way of talking about it. Unquestionably, part of the reason for interpreting experiences in words is to tell somebody else about it. Human beings are relating animals, and they relate both themselves and information to other persons. Quite apart from communication, verbalizing also serves the purpose of clarifying what has happened in the mind of the one to whom it happened. Much of the talking that people do which does not seem to be directed to anybody in particular is probably being done for precisely this purpose. It really doesn't matter much whether there is a listener or not. One suspects that many books have been written primarily for this purpose, with varying degrees of success. Further, putting experiences into words is a way of seeking the meaning in that which is not understood. Man feels, deep within him, that if he can only force the event or the insight into the little boxes that words provide and line them up in the sequences grammar insists upon, he will have some hold on the meaning of it. Verbalizing is therefore also a method, not merely for reflecting, but for seeking meaning. Many of the sentences of philosophers are logical exercises, games played with words in the effort to locate and establish truth.

Theology is precisely such a meaning-seeking, truth-clarifying, significance-communicating undertaking. In that sense, it is a discipline not much different from science or logic. The experience it verbalizes is, however, distinctive. Because God is one agent in the divine-human dialogue, theology is doomed to a certain degree of ineptitude. Not only is the experience itself ineffable in that it is impossible to represent it adequately in words; God is not describable in sense based words because he does not present himself to the ordinary senses of sight and sound and touch. When words must be used to describe the encounter with God, a mathematician like Pascal is reduced to a single word, "Fire!" which is surely not a literal description. A mystic like Paul is driven to describing a "voice" which no one else heard. A dialectician like Kierkegaard is forced to beat his head against the wall of Hegelian logic "until the blood runs." In the service of theology words are strained to the breaking point and are forced to perform wonders no other discipline asks of them. No wonder Horace Bushnell exclaimed, "The poets are the best metaphysicians."

Theology is not really a lost cause, however, though it has seemed so to some. Because God is one agent in the divine-human dialogue, there is always a constant factor in the religious experiences of men. The invitation is always the same: it comes from God, who is the same "yesterday and today and for ever." The purpose is always the same: it is the salvation of man from selfishness, alienation, and anxiety. The motive is always the same: it is the personal love of God who created human beings for the sake of each of them personally. And, because the other agent in the divine-human dialogue is always man, there is another constant, if infinitely more unpredictable, factor. Human beings differ universally but they do not differ absolutely. There are basic characteristics of organic structure and thought patterns that render men a definable species, which means that men resemble one another more than they differ from one another. Through the centuries the evidence piles up and an identifiable core makes itself recognizable.

For all these reasons, theology is for Christians one of the most fascinating and rewarding of disciplines as well as a necessity. It seeks, clarifies, and communicates the meaning of the divine-human dialogue. Every teacher of Christianity is, at his own level of competence, a theologian. Being the best possible teacher also means being the best possible theologian. Considering the subject, only his best is good enough.

*

Theology has three primary tasks: to seek, to clarify, and to communicate.

Theology *seeks the meaning* of the divine-human dialogue in the human experience of it. Through the ages, men have tried to tell about their own experiences of God's acts. A large number of these reports, written over the span of a thousand years, has been brought together in the Bible. It is recognized by Christians as a very special record of what has happened when God speaks to man and man rebels or responds. The New Testament report is that God entered history and personally confronted man face-to-face, self-to-self, as man, and implies that God was not only involved in the being of Jesus of Nazareth but also in some way participated in his life, death, and resurrection, specifically identifying himself with men, revealing his divine love, and showing his "human face." Through the centuries since, Christians have continued to write about their encounters with God, some biographically, some theologically, some devotionally. Others have not written about their experiences, but have reflected the dialogue in their lives. Some say that they have found God in the lives of all men, imperfect and finite, good or evil though they may be. Others witness that God discloses himself in the order, awe, and sometimes fury of the physical universe. The Bible, Jesus Christ, and the reports and lives of those who have been convinced personally of the results of the reality of the divine-human dialogue provide a rich resource in which theology seeks for the meaning of it.

Another source is the interpretations of those experiences and the formalizing of them into doctrines. Doctrines have been formulated differently in different ages and reflect the needs and nature of the times. In the New Testament period, Christian doctrine was very simple, reflecting the impatience of the early Christian with this world, his expectation of its imminent end, and his personal memory of Jesus. In the third century, Christian doctrine reflected the demand of the Greek mind for clear-cut, arithmetic precision. In the Middle Ages, Christian doctrine reflected the immobility, superstition, and stratification of feudal society. In the sixteenth century, Christian doctrine reflected the Reformers' rejection of earthly authority, their reliance on the Bible, and their sense of God's immediate presence and directing will. In the nineteenth century, Christian doctrine showed the influence of the industrial society, the evolutionary hypothesis, and the general optimism of the day. In their varied and common reference to the certainty of divine love and its singular concretion in Jesus Christ, together with its results in and for human living, the Christian doctrines provide a second source in which theology seeks for the meaning of the divine-human dialogue.

Theology also attempts to *clarify the meaning* of the divine-human dialogue. Of course, it has not always seemed so. The history of Christianity has been famous for its sometimes spectacular and often bitter quarrels about the meaning of it all. Arius and Athanasius battled with each other about the nature of the incarnation until the public riots and the bawdy songs determined Constantine to call a council of churchmen from all over the Empire to settle the quarrel and restore unity. There was a scandalous amount of log-rolling and string-pulling, judging from reports, but the result was the Nicene Creed, which managed not only to diminish the tumult but also to state the essence of the matter—Jesus Christ was "wholly man and wholly God." The Emperor sought a compromise in a quarrel and he got a clarification out of a dispute. Theological understanding has often been refined in the fires of controversy. The sheer, stubborn, relentless give and take of differing conviction has been one of the ways in which theologians are encouraged to say what they mean and to mean what they say. The disputation in medieval universities made formal use of the method. Contemporary theologians use discussion among colleagues and with students. Controversy may get out of hand, of course, at the cost of bad blood and spilled blood among men who ought to have been behaving as brothers.

When contained by love, however, it is one of the tools of theological clarification. Not only meaning but dialogue itself ought to be found when it is.

Another way of clarification takes place in the arena of one's own mind. The tools are the traditional tests of rational logic: coherence, consistency, and comprehensiveness. More recent philosophical discussion has concentrated on the nature of language itself as supplying the key to clarity. Much of what theologians and their traditional philosophical colleagues had been saying seemed to many of a more scientific and technical turn of mind to be confused and woolly. Indeed, it did sometimes seem that theologians, both those of the professionally philosophical sort and those who spoke more directly to the people from pulpits, tended to talk, if not sheer nonsense, at least a kind of language that was chiefly obscure and irrelevant. Even the vocabulary seemed hopelessly archaic and unnecessarily multi-syllabled. Many who became discouraged with the church as well as many who remained loyal churchmen decided that theology had little to do with the urgent matters of living. Theology owes it to itself to be clear, and an understanding of the way both scientific and spiritual language works is one of the theologian's tools. The difficulty, of course, is that theology is not describing technical and objective physical realities so much as living and personal spiritual realities. Indeed, the ultimate language of theology is not a language in the ordinary sense, but a Person. The Word of God to men is not contained in the symbols of any human speech, but in the personal incarnation of God in Christ. One of the constant tasks of theology is to learn how to use that personal language effectively.

Theology also attempts to *communicate the meaning* of the divine-human dialogue. Sometimes professional theologians have not given much evidence that they thought communication was part of their task. They have sometimes secreted themselves in monasteries and libraries. They have sometimes seemed preoccupied solely with abstract definition. They have sometimes joined other Christians in stoning prophets and silencing visionaries. They have sometimes seemed to prefer obscurity to the obvious and vagueness to the vivacious. And sometimes, overeager to communicate, they have merely reflected the non-Christian world about them.

However, theologians have also offered their insight into the nature of God and their judgment upon sin to the world in unmistakable terms. They have fearlessly proclaimed the righteousness of God to dissipated Florentine nobles, challenged a dissolute church to purify itself, called Hitler demonic. Such theologians are the first to acknowledge that in a real engagement with the world Christianity risks losing some of its familiar formulas and ways of thinking. If the meaning of the divine-human dialogue is to be spoken effectively to the world, Christians must be constantly on the search for new words and symbols in which to embody their faith, new ways of reaching through to touch the life of the world. To do this they need to be secure enough in their theology to be able to change its forms and purge its errors, certain enough of its heritage to develop and project it.

Theology consists of seeking, clarifying, and communicating the meaning of the divine-human dialogue. These functions are not carried on separately, of course, and theologians are forever discovering that as they pursue a point it becomes clearer, as they communicate their understanding it is both clarified and supplemented, as they struggle for clarity they achieve effectiveness.

*　　*

In the disciplines of theology, the teacher of Christianity finds the clue for dealing with theology in the teaching-and-learning process: theology is learned by theologizing. Theology is most effectively learned and taught as the experience of divine-human dialogue is sought, clarified, and communicated.

Theology is learned as the meaning of the divine-human dialogue is actively sought. In teaching both the Bible and Christian history, the teacher of Christianity is teaching the basic sources of theology —the records and accounts of human responses to the divine address across the ages. The first lessons in theology for most laymen are ordinarily biographical, and they begin with hearing the stories of the Bible and of the Christian heroes. A more systematic and thorough search of the records of dialogue might be the proper place for an adolescent or adult class to begin the study of theology.

Instruction in theology should also include a study of the doctrines that have arisen as an attempt to formalize these experiences. The learner of Christianity should be led through the major doctrines: Creation and Revelation, God, the Person and Work of Christ, the Holy Spirit, the Trinity, Sin and Salvation, the Church, Personal and Social Ethics, Last Things. He should trace their changes and be aware of the variegated pressures that have influenced their development. He should become acquainted with some of the heresies. He should be helped to see that what has been called "orthodoxy" is not a hard line so much as a firm ground, that it is not so much a pipeline as a stream flowing a winding course between wide and marshy banks and accepting water from many tributaries. This is often an excellent study for older adolescents, in or out of college, who have some knowledge of history.

Theology is also learned in attempts to clarify the meaning of one's own religious experience. This is one of the favorite occupations of adolescents, and the teacher of Christianity may be quite certain that the process is going on, whether or not he enlists it in the teaching-and-learning of theology. Christians need help in finding a vocabulary with which to express their feelings and convictions.

That they tend to be reluctant to talk about them is more an indication of illiteracy than of irreligiousness. Their tongues need to be freed by discovering a vocabulary. One sort of theological language is traditional, and Christians need to learn it and be able to use it. This is not an unreasonable suggestion, for most laymen have already learned several special vocabularies, one for the job, one for recreation, and one for social occasions. Christians should be introduced to the long and classic words of Christian doctrine. They have very definite meanings and are not frightening when understood: Atonement, Baptism, Crucifixion, Divinity; Eschatology, Faith, Grace, Hope; Incarnation, Justification, Koinonia, Love; Mediation, Numinous, Omnipresence, Providence; Reconciliation, Sacrament, Teleology, Unction, Vocation, and even *Weltanschauung*. Every Christian should have a working word list of a hundred specifically Christian words, knowing something about their meaning, their historic usages, their theological implications. It is no secret that the best way to teach and learn words is by using them.

Theology is also learned in the attempt to communicate it. Any classic theological word list tends to be jargon until it is explored and worked. To be useful in communication, it needs translation. The language of Christianity is not objective and scientific, but personal. Its chief statement is not a sentence but a life. The language of Christianity, which wrestles with the problem of putting into words the acts of a personal God, is a personal language. It will use words with which persons are familiar as persons. It will probably be the language of ordinary speech about personal affairs, used at its richest and with precision. It is composed largely of words about relationships, like "communion," "fellowship," "love," and other words like "alienation," "isolation," "judgment." These are more than words, they are symbols for the experiences of being personal, of speaking and answering in the dialogue of human existence. They are also religious words, for they describe God's personal relation to human persons. The specifically Christian affirmation is that God comes to men through his Son, Jesus Christ. The words of personal relationship can, with care and consistency, be enlisted to carry this meaning, also. An important way of teaching-and-learning theology is to work out a personal, twentieth-century glossary for the classic theological vocabulary and to practice using it, especially with those who do not understand or accept the old-fashioned words.

At every level, theology is learned by active seeking, clarifying, and communicating. This is learning-by-doing. There is no better way.

*   *   *

Christianity is a tradition to be known, a stance to be selected, a way of life to be lived. As learners actively seek to know the tradition, attempt to clarify the stance they have selected, and try to communicate a way of life by living it, the experience of divine-human dialogue is enabled. As learners participate in the dialogue, theology is created.

21

Teaching with Music

Music is a form of dialogue and provides an appropriate accompaniment for the teaching of Christianity.

All art is in the nature of dialogue. Painting is an address by the artist, out of his experience with the world and his vision of it, through the colors and shapes and lines of his painting, to an observer

194

who responds by finding in the painting an insight about the nature of his own experience of the world. Dialogue, of which art is a form, is the process of creating participation, making mutual what had been isolated and singular. Art achieves this meeting through the agency of an artifact. Teaching enables dialogue through a personal crossing over to the learner's side of experience. Religion is a sharing reached through the risk of address and the adventure of response. Christianity, of which all these forms are approximations, accomplishes the meeting of God and man through the person of Jesus Christ.

Music has always been linked with religion. Drums sent the shamans into ecstasy, and many primitive peoples think the drum is filled with spirits. Nietzsche said that rhythm constrains the gods. Plato rejected all music because of its irrational power, but he especially distrusted martial music. Pacific Islanders suppose the flute speaks with the voice of a spirit. When Ambrose introduced hymn singing into the worship at Milan in the fourth century, he was accused of occultism. The bishop acknowledged the mystic power of music but not the charge: "What can be more powerful," he argued, "than the confession of the Trinity by the mouth of the entire people?" Ambrose took his stand on ancient ground. "My heart is steadfast," wrote the Hebrew psalmist, "I will sing and make melody." In the heavenly city which the Revelation of John describes, the final thing is song. Though Calvin rejected most of the trappings of Rome, he retained song, for both biblical and practical reasons: he knew that people must sing and preferred to have the sounds of joy in church. The Lutherans turned chorales into marching songs for the Reformation. And when the Puritans purged themselves of beauty, they retained a form, though deliberately not very beautiful, of music. Music is today the traditional art form among Protestants. In many parts of the world dominated by Catholicism or paganism, the most distinctive Protestant witness is not a magnificent building or the pastor-scholar or laymen in influential places, but a singing congregation.

Music is so much a part of the Protestant ethos and so directly related by its nature to the educative dialogue, that it is almost inconceivable that the teaching-and-learning of Christianity could proceed without its constant accompaniment.

*

Music is a form of dialogue in which everyone can participate.

Experienced music teachers say that there is no person who cannot sing. The child who drones along on a single pitch is probably neither absolutely tone-deaf nor unable to produce different tones. The chances are that he whistles well enough. The adult who feels that he cannot sing has probably never been shown how and is now so embarrassed about his incapacity that he has learned the socially acceptable way of refusing to try. The problem is coordination between hearing pitches and the rather complex physical actions producing them. Music teachers know how to teach the necessary coordination. However, most people can and do sing, at war, in the bath, on the job, and even seriously.

On the other hand, singing that is rewarding is not easily accomplished. It is a highly disciplined art form. It calls into play a sophisticated combination of skills blending a sensitivity to pitch and an awareness of rhythm, together with the ability to employ diaphragm, lungs, larynx, and resonators in the production of sounds as beautiful and meaningful as possible, all added to the capacity to read notes and words from a page of symbols. In a very real way, as every great singer attests, the entire body from toe to scalp and all the powers of the mind participate in a united and controlled effort.

This combination of spontaneity and discipline is built up of many skills that are achieved gradually. Before the infant begins to talk, he learns to distinguish sounds and gradually to imitate them. The first imitation is usually of rhythm and is achieved by large physical movements. Later, he will learn to match pitch. Therefore, by the time the child comes to the preschool class, he enjoys clapping, thumping and marching, humming, squeaking and roaring. To do these things together with other children can be one of his first and most valuable experiences of dialogue. Later will come the fun of musical games, the unity of marching, the excitement of free movement to music. There is no reason that children should not do all these things to the praise of God in their worship.

By the primary age, children can begin to learn to sing. There is a real thrill in producing a single clear pitch together, and it has to do with the spiritual experience of dialogue. The tunes are made up of simple and repetitive sequences of notes. They fall within a four- or five-tone range. The words are simple and have to do with familiar experiences. They fall naturally to the rhythms of the music. Most of the songs are learned by rote from following the teacher, but the children will invent some of their own. These songs, too, should become part of their worship occasions.

By middle childhood, children can learn to read music. If they have not been taught in school, the church should be able and ready. Each child might be given his own hymnbook, exactly as many churches give Bibles as a sign of basic work accomplished and as a hope of continued use. By later childhood, children can learn to sing harmonies. Their voices can be trained, taking advantage of native gifts and improving poor quality. The children are ready to form choirs which rehearse regularly, and share in the leadership of formal worship.

Other forms of musical participation, from listening to recorded music to learning to play instruments, will develop together with learning to sing. All along, and with everyone participating, music is both a form and expression of the experience of dialogue.

*   *

Music provides a natural medium for the meeting of adults and children.

In our superbly organized society, there is an age-grouping process working everywhere. School children spend half their waking time with other children whose ages differ no more than a few months from their own. In large school systems, due to the fad for talent grouping, they will associate only with children whose I.Q.s are within a dozen points of their own. Adolescents spend so much of their time together that they develop a slanguage so distinctive that their parents sometimes cannot understand them. Working men become so thoroughly adjusted to the thought patterns and vocabulary of their colleagues that they find it difficult to associate with anyone else.

Meeting across these barriers is a creative achievement, educating both participants in the dialogue. Music, especially group singing, provides a bridge. It has often served that function in the past. The Moravian movement, as reported by Zinzendorf, used choirs as one of its chief educational and communal functions. Everyone in the community, from youngest to oldest, was in a choir of his own age. The choir was more than a musical organization in which songs were rehearsed and learned; it was also a Bible study unit, which is interesting to modern churchmen, not so much for its blending of biblical theme and song, which was often bizarre, as for its achievement of togetherness. All the choirs met regularly together, to hear one another sing and to sing with one another. In the New England Singing School, everyone in the village, from child to adult, was taught the rudiments of sightsinging as the basis for singing together. The Spirituals of the Negroes not only provided a perspective on their suffering but bound the generations together. In the late nineteenth century, many a family made music together on Sunday afternoons in the sitting room. Music was the medium of meeting, and often adult met child in the simple but demanding business of mastering the techniques of the instrument and of reading the music.

*   *   *

Music is a natural medium for the meeting of past and present.

Music yields authentic insight into the nature of man, the nature of the beyond, and the nature of their relationship. Insofar as it is true, the insight is timeless, and so is the music that embodies it. One of the primary tasks of the teacher of Christianity is to make the past real, and music is a means to that end. However, music is not merely another means of saying something that may be equally well said in other ways. In the words of some musicians, music is not to be used programmatically. It is more than an illustration, even though it does say some things very well. It is more than a teaching aid, a trick to be pulled out of the Standard Issue Teaching Kit when a special effect is needed, even though the immediate effect of music as a fascinator for wool-gathering adolescents and a pacifier for insecure four-year-olds is well known.

When performed, music is entirely in the present and speaks for itself. It is heard *now*. But it literally calls across from the composer's experience to the listener's; it speaks to ears not the composer's own. This capacity of a single composition to create moods and evoke pictures more or less similar to those the composer was working with has been much discussed. However, concert or program music illustrating moods and themes is not so much the concern of the teacher of Christianity as the informal, celebrational music of the people that sprang unbidden and often unplanned from a distant culture's experience. Every culture has its own forms of musical expression, and they reflect the culture, the values, the problems, and the joys that have combined to make that culture distinctive. In every period Christians have developed their own musical forms, and enough of them are still available to comprise a rich resource. The teacher is interested, first, in the objective fact that a Hebrew chant or medieval song has arisen out of a religious tradition and cultural setting and can be taken to be an honest and authentic expression of experience. He is interested, secondly, in the mysterious fact that hearing—or, even better, recreating—that music in the present stirs into being a response to experience authentically similar to that of the ancient musician.

It is the opportunity of this passage across time, narrow and tenuous but direct and immediate, to the other side of a distant and different experience, that music provides. The teacher will not merely illustrate the Reformation with a few snatches of German chorale and Genevan psalm tune dropped incidentally into the lesson period. He will rather seek ways of teaching the Reformation to the accompaniment of Reformation music.

*　　*　　*　　*

Training in musicianship is an appropriate occupation for the church.

Musical training is steadily becoming less available in other parts of the community. In the rush to crowd more mathematics and science into the curriculum, public schools are quietly eliminating frills, froth, and fun. In many communities, both large and small, the private teacher of music is disappearing. At the same time, in more and more churches, there is a minister of music, usually on a part-time basis, who ekes out the rest of his living at some other occupation he enjoys less. At the church building there are a half-dozen pianos deteriorating from disuse, an organ silent for all but two or three hours a week, and rooms standing vacant between

Sunday noon and Sunday morning. In this combination of conditions, there may be a rare opportunity for the church to seize leadership in enabling a basically religious form of artistic experience.

Let the minister of music become a full-time member of the church staff, giving lessons all week long in the church building and using the church equipment. The tuition and rental fees paid by the students could be paid directly into the church treasury. The church musician would give singing lessons, individually and in small groups. Instrumental lessons would also be available. Choirs and ensembles would be created for all age groups, talent levels, and interests. From morning to night the church buildings would be filled with the sound of music of all kinds—sacred, classical, folk, pop, and jazz.

In the church school, music would become a part of every unit of study. There would be a supply of record players and a library of materials. Teachers would be informed of the opportunities for integrating music with their teaching. Some teachers would specialize in teaching songs to specific age groups and in a knowledge of the appropriate materials. Either in the classes or in additional sessions, they would sing together. The learning of new hymns would be a regular practice throughout the church, together with something of their history and technical construction. The minister of music would himself become a consultant to the educational program of the church, providing materials, advice, and supervision.

There is probably no form of group discipline more challenging than music. There can be no ensemble without every voice at its best and most consistent. Patience is required for those who are not technically adept. Rehearsals must begin and end on time. Everything is focused on the group achievement. Love and grace are constantly being called into exercise, but they are not cheap and easy. And when the ensemble has been achieved, there is perhaps no greater flight of the human spirit enabled by the human spirit than that borne aloft on the sound of group music one is himself helping to create. Dialogue is, in spirit and in fact, in rehearsal.

Periodically, this training and effort converge upon a single event. The entire community gathers, and with a conscious pooling of their talents and practice, they offer their music in joyous celebration of their presence together in the presence of God. Teaching with music has overflowed into worship.

*

Music is a natural and effective accompaniment for the teaching of Christianity. The art of teaching and learning music lies very close to the teaching of Christianity. If the church will provide the training in the basic skills hand in hand with its teaching-and-learning of dialogue, music can become the audible texture binding past to present, child to adult, and man to God.

22

Teaching Teachers

Enabling teachers to enable dialogue is the key to keeping the teaching-and-learning process alive and meaningful.

From the point of view of the educational process, learners are the heart of the teaching-and-learning dialogue. From the point of view of scholarship, content is central. But from the point of view of strategy, teachers are the key. If a dozen teachers are interested and interesting, it is probable that a dozen classes will be interesting and a dozen-dozen learners will be interested. For the maintenance and improvement of educational excellence, the teaching staff must be kept alive and alert.

In the first half of the twentieth century, this principle has produced in the United States a vast system of state-supported teachers' colleges. At mid-century, distinguished studies of state-controlled education have emphasized the importance of raising the academic and intellectual standards of teacher-training institutions as the first element of any plan for meeting the unprecedented demands of the post-war world on education. In the churches, there have been various plans for improving the quality of church school teaching. Councils of Churches have sponsored teacher-training courses on an ecumenical basis, attempting to provide for each church the best instruction available from the community at large. Denominational programs have tended to concentrate on textbooks and manuals for teachers, designed to accompany the courses they are currently teaching. Nevertheless, some church leaders, noting the continuing low level of church school teaching and despairing therefore of programs for helping volunteer teachers, have urged that teachers of Christianity be paid for their services. It is easy, in a materialistic and secular culture, to suppose that salaries and equipment will somehow automatically produce competent teaching. This is the reason, presumably, that when any criticism is made of the public schools, from low literacy to losing football teams, the School Board almost invariably replies that "salaries are too low," and "the buildings are inadequate." However, though church school facilities are everywhere open to criticism, often on the grounds of serious educational inadequacy, mere professionalism is not the cure-all answer to the problems of teaching Christianity. Indeed, it may be no answer at all, for dialogue is not taught professionally. The essence of

Christianity can only be taught by the amateur, that is, by the person who does it for love, as the root word "amare" suggests. Paychecks, especially small ones, tend to obscure that basic fact. The basis for an appropriate strategy lies much deeper than budget. The teacher of Christianity must, indeed, be given reason to know that what he is doing is important and matters to many people. He must be provided with facilities which both emphasize the importance of his work and support it. Most important, however, he needs to be continuously in dialogue with a teacher, with the content, and with other learners.

Teachers teach best as they are taught. The evidence from all teacher-training programs is almost unanimous about two points: teachers tend to teach most naturally in the same manner in which they were themselves taught; they tend to teach at their own best while they are themselves being taught. The first point is sometimes said by the educational progressivists to account for the resistance to change in educational methods. As long as lecturing is the primary teaching method of teachers' colleges, they say, students of teachers' colleges will lecture when they teach. Parish ministers tend to specialize in monologues because, when they were in theological school, the teaching-and-learning process was largely monological. Church school teachers almost always tend to conduct their classes—no matter what they have been told about other teaching methods—in the same manner in which Aunt Martha taught them when they were primary children a third of a century ago. The second point is one of the primary reasons for "practice teaching" and "laboratory school" techniques pioneered by teachers' colleges. Usually, the best teaching a public school teacher has ever done was that accomplished as a student teacher during his training. There seem to be two reasons: he was simultaneously being exposed to new content matter himself, and he was made conscious of the learners' side of experience by being himself a learner while teaching.

In these observations is implied what may be the most effective strategy for teaching teachers of Christianity.

*

Before teachers even begin to teach, they must, of course, be recruited.

Securing teachers for classes in Christianity is often a haphazard and thoughtless affair, almost surely designed, it would seem, to frighten away the best material and recruit the worst, except for the mysterious goodness of heart that sometimes leads good people to teach, regardless. "Now, who will I ever get for that class of third-grade monsters? . . . Oh, there's Mrs. Jones! I never thought of her, probably because I don't know her at all. . . . Oh, hello, Betty Jones I'm so glad I happened to see you. . . . Oh, how dreadful, excuse me, Margaret. . . . Well, I wonder if you would like to—well, if you would—teach the third-grade class this fall. . . . Oh, no, just this one term; we'll find somebody else by next spring, I'm sure. . . . The course is easy—it's just about the Life of Jesus—and the teachers' manual tells you just everything to do so it won't take much time for preparation. . . ." Other recruitment programs begin by searching the files of church members for people who are, or have ever been, public school teachers ("after all, they *know* how to teach, don't they?") without ever inquiring about their real interests and gifts.

According to the view that teaching-and-learning Christianity is the enabling of a human answer to the divine address by exposing the learner to illustrations and experiences of dialogue, the most promising recruit is the person who is himself open to dialogue—an eager, responsive, openhearted, growing human being. He is, therefore, basically a "religious person." This much is essential. The very capacity to respond is probably the best invitation to response one human being can make to another. If he already understands the Christian convictions about the interhuman and the divine-human dialogue, so much the better. He probably also possesses some qualities of earnestness, conscientiousness, reliability. They will all be useful in teaching. He needs to have some intelligence, and probably does; he does not need to be highly educated, and if he is, the nature of his education and his use of it in his own thinking will probably have much to say about the class and content he should be offered. If he has the capacity and the interest to become a specialist in some field of Christian knowledge, he may be recruited to pursue those matters in view of future teaching. His love and concern will be his primary qualifications, however; having these, other qualities that produce the effective teacher can be developed. He will be recruited because he is a person, and he will be recruited to be a person in the classroom.

This kind of recruit is everywhere. Some of the more sensitive of them tend to stand aloof from the institutional church and its programs. They are easily hurt by being "used," and are quickly discouraged by programs that limit their freedom and clamp a tight lid on possibilities. They are nonetheless Christian for these attitudes. An excellent territory for recruitment of teachers of Christianity is the periphery of the church's programs.

An essential part of recruitment is the assurance of support in the actual teaching-and-learning situation. Teaching in the church school tends to be one of the loneliest jobs known to man: week after week a teacher can come to the church building on Sunday morning, scurry down the long hall to his own dark cubicle, agonize with teaching a lesson no one has ever discussed with him through a period constantly interrupted with announcements and explanations from a headquarters he does not really know, dismiss the class, tidy up the room, and slink back home without ever encountering anything but other lonely shadows in the hallway. If persons are to be brought into the church school, especially sensitive, conscientious, and growing persons, they ought to have evidence in advance that they will be treated and supported as persons involved in an important and challenging task.

The best possible recruitment device is a known program for teaching teachers.

*   *

The best training of leaders for the teaching-and-learning of Christianity is a continuous exposure to the quest for dialogue. It begins no later than the first day the child enters the Kindergarten Department. It continues through all the classes the prospective leader ever attends as a child and adolescent. It is felt in the committee work and group planning he does as a member of the community. It is present in the worship and fellowship occasions of the church life. In addition to this general preparation, however, the teacher needs constant exposure to the content of teaching-and-learning and the dialogue of teaching-and-learning itself. For the dialogue to live, the teacher must also continuously be a learner.

The first and indispensable element of continuous dialogue for the teacher is tutorial: face-to-face, week-by-week sessions with a teacher of his own. The tutor has probably had some experience in teaching the material or the age group the teacher-learner is now working with, but it is not necessary for him to be a "master" teacher. His task is to support and assist the enabler of dialogue by offering dialogue to him. The session may begin with the question: "How did your class go last week?" Ordinarily, the teacher-learner will be encouraged to review the session in detail, reporting actual comments and events. It is usually good practice for the tutor never to visit the class which is being reported; the simple fact that the tutor is totally dependent upon the teacher's report for information will encourage the teacher to be observant and honest. The teacher will criticize his own reactions and contributions, but self-evaluation is not the heart of the review. He will be urged, rather, to understand their meaning in regard to the pupil's response to address. The teacher-of-teachers may suggest methods of handling the material for next week. He and the teacher-learner may go over the content together. The tutor will often have new resources to suggest. They may be read together. They may make lesson plans together. Whatever is done will be done for the purpose of offering the teacher-learner an experience of dialogue from which to work in his own effort to enable dialogue for his learners. There can be no mere imitation of the tutor or his methods, just because the teacher's class situation is so very different. "Each one teach one" has been a classic strategy of the Christian movement, and lies at the root of dialogue. With this experience every week, the teacher will go to his class ready for face-to-face meeting.

The second indispensable element in teacher-teaching is a good library. It will contain reference volumes to supplement the teacher's materials. There will be other curriculum materials available for comparison and study. There will be books of teaching methods. The picture file, the catalogue of films and slides, the maps and models and time lines will be there. The tutorial session may well take place in this room. If not, the teacher will be acquainted with the library's resources and encouraged in every possible way to make use of it.

The teacher-learner will also be provided with ample opportunities to develop his own Christian understanding. There should be regular courses in which the school's teachers can sit together as learners. These may deal with two kinds of material: content and teaching methods. Every teacher should have opportunity to go more deeply into the whole subject matter of the Christian movement and faith. He should be enrolled, now and then, in classes which have no direct relation to the content he is teaching himself: he needs all the background and perspective he can get. He should also do some courses in the specific subject-matter he is called upon to teach: he cannot become too knowledgeable about it. Occasionally, he should have the opportunity to study teaching methods and age-group psychology as well as content. It would be helpful for the teacher to be able to study the ages just above and just below that of the class he is now teaching. More good would probably be accomplished by one hour spent weekly in such learning than most teachers achieve in an hour of preparation by themselves, but it is no substitute for individual preparation.

The teacher-learner should also have opportunity to meet other teachers, personally. These occasions may be formal, with business and agenda, but this is not a substitute for personal acquaintance. The best meetings are informal, with free, sometimes one-to-one conversation and fellowship. They need not, however, be frequent or extended. A place and fifteen minutes for informal gathering and talk just after the day's sessions, for example, may be more effective than regular, planned activities and extended monthly meetings.

Other familiar programs may be utilized: observation, supervision, and team teaching; institutes, conferences, and conventions; correspondence schools, teacher training courses, laymen's schools. The heart of the program, however, important enough to be regularly and earnestly maintained, is the tutorial program: it is the dialogical relationship between a teacher-of-teachers and a teacher-learner that keeps dialogue alive and growing. This is usually the task of the minister or the trained director of education in the local church. It may be difficult for him to do this, particularly if his own theological education did not give him a personal experience of tutorial relation. It will be time-consuming, of course, but if he will be bold enough to claim one-third of his working week for this purpose and devote fifty minutes to each teacher, he may regularly tutor a dozen to a score. He may find it necessary to choose where to begin. In time, some will be able to offer this tutorial dialogue to others, and a chain-reaction will have been released. Even at the beginning, he will be doing something directly creative for a dozen classes every week, which is more than many ministers seem to have done in far more than a week.

*

Dialogue is enabled by entering into dialogue. Teachers teach best as they are taught. The minister is called upon to become a teacher-of-teachers. Of course, to take these principles seriously and to act upon them conscientiously is to run the risk that the power of the Christian experience may grow in the community of teaching-and-learning.

23

The Christian Revolution

If the existing agencies for teaching-and-learning Christianity were to concentrate on enabling dialogue, the long-prepared Christian revolution would flower almost immediately.

To call the Christian movement revolutionary is only, of course, to state a fact. Very early its agents were accused of turning the world upside down. It is not, however, the fashion to mention it often. The appearance of a conscious counterrevolution on the scene of world history ought to have brought the revolutionary nature of Christianity out into the open. The great opportunity for Christianity is to out-revolutionize Marxism. The reaction of Christians in general, however, seems to have been to assume that maintenance of the status quo, though admitted to fall far short of God's intent for the life of man, is the only alternative to revolution. The implication is that communism is the only valid revolution there is.

The revolution Christianity aims at is not violent. It is not materialistic. It is, however, total. Christians believe that the presence of God in human life is so potent and that his will for human life is so creative that if it were taken seriously, the entire world would be refashioned. They think that God is actively at work in human history, constantly addressing man in love and in grace, enabling the sort of response that would eventually create a new world. They see the possibility implanted within human nature of construction rather than destruction, of cooperation rather than competition, of trust rather than suspicion, of concern rather than power, of peace rather than war. They see the possibility that, released from the necessity of self-centeredness and defensiveness, men might cooperate to solve the problems of needless disease, illiteracy, water and food shortages, population explosion, poverty. They hold the dream that, in a world of human beings responding to God in love and joy, there may be no need for regulation and prescription, punishment and reward. God will be present and his will acknowledged in the affairs of men.

Sometimes Christians have not acted as if they believe these things at all. They have withdrawn from life, persecuted deviationists, grown fat and satisfied and dull. They have all too often smothered the spirit of dialogue. But they have at other times remembered

213

that Jesus offered the gift of the living address of God wherever he was, and that the poor rather than the rich, the common rather than the successful, the oppressed rather than the rulers tended to be the ones who responded. They remember that he won his followers one-by-one, in face-to-face personal dialogue, and that, ever since, the direct impact of one who knows and cares upon one who does not has been the basic strategy of Christians. Thus the revolution the Christian seeks will probably come slowly, like the growth of a plant from a seed, imperceptibly like the leavening of a loaf of bread by a bit of yeast. Its method will probably be the same as its goal: the quiet changing of the loyalties and behavior of individuals, one by one. The facilities for achieving this revolution in one generation are at hand.

*

According to widely accepted statistics, forty-one million children and adolescents attend Protestant church schools every week in the United States alone. From a space platform over Kansas City on a bright spring Sunday morning, this would be an impressive scene. Almost on signal, between a fifth and a fourth of the entire population moves out of its homes to the churches—rural, suburban, and inner city. The church buildings vary widely in size and style, but many of them have excellent modern schoolroom buildings, and most of them have at least several classrooms especially equipped for education. In practically all these hundreds of thousands of classrooms, there are tables, chairs, blackboards, maps, and pictures. In many of them, movies and slides will be shown. For almost every student there are elegantly illustrated and carefully composed textbooks, rivaling in scholarship and teachability those of the public schools. Some three million adults, most of them volunteers, will be there as teachers and administrators, and most of them have been offered some training for their work.

It is to be expected that in some of the classrooms the children's activities do not seem to have much to do with the Christian faith. Some of the classes are poorly taught by teachers who have not taken advantage of the training offered them. Too many of the teachers do not seem to understand the importance of what they are doing. In many places, the young people appear to be bored and rebellious. Some of the discussions of biblical passages do not seem very meaningful.

However, all these millions of learners and teachers have some sort of confidence that if one knows the biblical story, the life, death, and resurrection of Jesus Christ, the history of the Christian movement, and the basic tenets of its faith, God will be known personally, and individuals will respond in their own ways to God's acts of love. So, whether well-taught or poorly, they troop home expecting to come again next week.

* *

This Sunday program is, however, only part of the educational program of the Christian movement. It is, literally, a weekwide and lifelong program, enlisting some of the greatest scholars and teachers of the era, capable of leading the learner to any depth he is willing and able to go. The total program of teaching-and-learning opportunities offered by the Christian movement comprises a Christian collegium, reaching from the bottom to the top of life.

For fifty years, the church school in the United States has been striving to find more time for its educational program than Sunday morning permits. Building on the methods of the Sunday school and attempting primarily to reach the same ages of learners, the church has experimented with other programs. One experiment has been to hold classes on some other day than Sunday. Impressed with the remarkable success some Jewish congregations have had with Sunday morning Synagogue schools, some Protestant educators have held schools on Saturday morning. Others have tried hours after public school dismissal during the week. The coming of post-war affluence, with weekend family trips and after-school dancing and piano lessons, has made it increasingly difficult to secure this additional time for religious education; some churches, however, have continued to have noteworthy success. Some churches have concentrated on using their facilities during the week for preschool education, for whom the public schools have no program. Many churches have utilized children's spare time during the long public school summer vacation and have made use of full or half days for three or four weeks. Another attempt has been to secure one period each week from the public school for religious instruction. In the United States, this attempt has been beset with thorny legal problems reared by the constitutional separation of church and state, and always there has been the awkwardness involved in permitting some children to absent themselves from the classes if they or their parents chose. In Great Britain, since the Education Act of 1944, religious instruction has been a part of the state school curriculum taught by professional teachers. In some American communities the program of released-time religious education has worked very well. Sometimes it has been possible to conduct these classes in school buildings; usually it has been necessary to move to a classroom off the campus; ordinarily the teachers are churchmen, not public school staff.

All these programs are designed for children and the giving of basic instruction in the Christian faith. This first exposure to the life of dialogue is of crucial importance and should be largely centered in actual experiences of dialogue. Of course, this kind of instruction also reaches upward into adolescent and adult ages and has its place there.

Another series of programs is designed primarily for learners of adolescent years. These usually concentrate on adding meaning to the basic setting and experience of the Christian dialogue. There are the regular courses offered chiefly on Sunday mornings and evenings. In most churches, the minister conducts special short courses of preparation for church membership. These usually supply review and summary for those young people who have come through the basic children's program. For those who have not, much of the material will be new. In addition, there are activity programs for young people in which the adolescent need for positive fellowship is experienced and explored. Weekend retreats, summer conferences, and work camps provide extended periods of time in which work and study are blended, sometimes with life-changing results.

The Christian movement also conducts courses at a high academic level in colleges and universities, theological seminaries and laymen's schools. These are designed for the student of late adolescent years and are usually open to adults as well. The concentration here tends to be on the objective content of the Christian scriptures, history, and philosophy. It enlists the talents of some of the world's most creative scholars, and a host of their protégés and interpreters in classrooms. In colleges and universities, religion courses are offered on a par with those of other subjects and in direct relation to them. In most of the church related colleges, some courses in religion are required for graduation, and in some state supported universities these courses are not only offered but draw large classes. Theological seminaries are professional schools, supported by the churches to produce scholars and pastors for the churches at all levels. They combine instruction in the practice of the ministry with scholarly study of Christianity at a graduate level, usually for full-time students but often open also to qualified laymen on a part-time basis. Laymen's schools are often conducted by the faculties of theological seminaries at special times and levels. Sometimes they are staffed by local ministers and administered by a Council of Churches.

Other parts of the Christian training program are designed for adults whose chief contact with Christianity is in local churches. They tend to concentrate on supplying basic background where it is needed, and on encouraging personal interpretation and application. In recent years, developing techniques for study and discussion of biblical passages in a context of personal intimacy and the sharing of problems and insights have made Bible study an exciting affair. There is a growing literature on the subject. They are usually under the guidance of volunteer laymen. It is a rare church now that does not have at least one study group meeting regularly, and usually the leadership has been trained in other parts of the educational program. Many churches also have seasonal programs of lectures and seminars, especially gathering about Advent and Lent. Denominational agencies provide a broad spectrum of retreats and study conferences, especially during holiday periods. Ordinarily a church headquarters staff provides the facilities, often an informal camping situation, designs the program, and secures the faculty. Some of them have developed special techniques for studying the Bible or the Life of Jesus, others for exploring social problems, and still others for nurturing the individual spiritual and devotional life.

In the local parish church, the regular services of worshiping and preaching nurture the life of dialogue and inform the mind, thus comprising a significant part of the training of the Christian movement. The work of the choirs, both in rehearsal and in presentation, is essentially educative. These activities are designed for the Christian community as a whole and tend to emphasize the practice of dialogue rather than the extension of the mind, but there is continuous opportunity in them for the teaching-and-learning of content.

* * *

All these activities comprise, by any account, a vast range of opportunities for teaching-and-learning Christianity. The Christian movement is, literally, an educational project with programs available for every level of interest and capacity throughout life. Though much of it is inept and inefficient, the scope of opportunities already existing tempts a vision of a local church consciously applied to making use of its programs and designed to house them and make them effective. It would probably look more like a campus than the usual church plant. In the morning, the library and research rooms will be in use by teachers preparing lessons and receiving tutorial instruction from senior faculty. In the afternoon, children will come after school hours for individual projects, music and art lessons, choirs, and small group classes. At meal times small groups of housewives and professional people will meet for discussion and study. There will be a bookstore, open regularly and operated on a minimum profit basis. At night, the lights will be burning in classrooms and rehearsal halls. The plant will be in use, every day and week in and week out.

On weekends, the pace would pick up noticeably, and on Sunday the entire facility would be in complete and continuous use. Families will come for the whole day. They will picnic together. There will be recreational facilities for use by all ages. Some will rest. There will be time for informal conversation and friendship. There will be a schedule of classes for all ages and interests, some of them purely elective. There will be worship at different times and of several different kinds. There may be regular, all-church events for a lecture or presentation of music, cinema, or drama.

The faculty will be both local laymen, professional staff, and visiting specialists. With simple living accommodations there could be a resident theologian of major standing, on leave from a seminary or after his retirement. On occasion, there might even be an artist-in-residence. Each teacher will also be simultaneously taking some of the other courses available.

Some local churches already possess most of the physical necessities for such a program. Others might need to build. If so, let the church consider the possibility of moving the church to the rural edge of town where space is more plentiful and less expensive, near a freeway exit and public transportation or the public school center, and create there a simple, functional conference ground for year-'round use. Let it even consider a site so attractive that church members would elect to build their own holiday and weekend retreats there. If the church cannot move or build, let it have the vision happening in its present situation and proceed to remodel to house this teaching-and-learning there.

*

The elements for total Christian training now exist in the teaching-and-learning programs of the Christian movement. The scholars are already at work, and the content is available in many excellent books. Enough buildings and the students are available. There is no practical reason that the Reformation dream of a literate people reading the Bible in their own way for their own salvation might not be here and now realized.

The mission of the teaching-and-learning of Christianity is simply to turn the ordinary values and practices of the world right side up. To accomplish it requires the most daring strategy, the most agonizing risk a human being can undertake—living and working with persons who may evade the opportunity of love, neither condoning nor condemning them for what they have been, identifying with them in their difficulties and achievements, offering to them the invitation to interhuman dialogue because God gave himself to man in much the same way. The facilities for accomplishing that Christian revolution lie already at hand. All that is necessary is to transform the equipment and the programs into a teaching-and-learning dialogue, bringing both teachers and learners into touch with the reality of God's presence and his inviting and enabling address.

We stand but a step—a generation—away from the most exciting and creative revolution history has known, but which, it seems, history has been intending all along. Perhaps no generation has had more to work with and less reason for not making use of it for the glory of God and the advancement of the redemptive revolution.

Bibliography

Barth, Karl. *The Word of God and the Word of Man.* Boston: The Pilgrim Press, 1928.

Brunner, Emil. *Truth as Encounter.* Philadelphia: The Westminster Press, 1964.

Buber, Martin. *Between Man and Man.* New York: The Macmillan Company, 1948.

———. *I and Thou.* New York: Scribner's, 1937.

Bushnell, Horace. *Christian Nurture.* New York: Scribner's, 1860.

Coe, George Albert. *What Is Christian Education?* New York: Scribner's, 1929.

Dewey, John. *Art as Experience*. New York: Minton (Putnam's), 1934.

————. *Democracy and Education*. New York: The Macmillan Company, 1916.

Kraemer, Hendrik. *Communication of the Christian Faith*. Philadelphia: The Westminster Press, 1956.

Macmurray, John. *Persons in Relation*. New York: Humanities Press, 1961.

————. *The Self as Agent*. New York: Harper, 1957.

————. *The Structure of Religious Experience*. London: Faber & Faber; 2nd ed., 1946.

Mehl, Roger. *La rencontre de l'autrui*. Neuchâtel: Delachaux & Niestlé, 1955.

Nida, Eugene. *Message and Mission*. New York: Harper, 1960.